Charting a Course to the Retirement of Your Dreams

Phillip Bell, CFP®
James K. "Skip" Nichols, ChFC, CLU
Donna Maddox, AIF®

www.TotalPublishingAndMedia.com

Copyright © 2020, Phillip Bell, CFP®, James K. "Skip" Nichols, ChFC, CLU, Donna Maddox, AIF®

All rights reserved.
No part of this book may be reproduced, stored in a retrieval system, or transmitted by any means, electronic, mechanical, photocopying, recording, or otherwise, without written permission from the author.

ISBN 978-1-63302-147-1

Dedication

We would like to dedicate this book to our wonderful families and to our amazing clients and their own families. Without all of you and your support, we would not be able to do what we do! Thank you for making Financial Planning Resources what is today. Our passion is teaching solid, principled concepts for money and life, and you make this possible.

Contents

Chapter 1: Your Dream of Retirement 1
Chapter 2: The Keys to Your Financial Independence 17
Chapter 3: Traps that Prevent Financial Independence 31
Chapter 4: Overcoming the Challenges of Retirement 37
Chapter 5: Assessing Your Financial Health 51
Chapter 6: How Much Do You Really Need? 65
Chapter 7: What to Do If You Don't Have Enough? 77
Chapter 8: The Saddest Things About Money 83
Chapter 9: The Fine Art of Getting Help 93
Chapter 10: Plan to Live the Highest Quality Life 105

Introduction

Our desire with this book is to help ensure the dream of retirement, no matter your background or the amount of planning you have done so far. Regardless of your economic bracket, whether you are blue collar or white collar, or how old you are as you read this, the book in your hand is like a roadmap. If you are well on your way, it will affirm your positive direction. And if you have gotten a little off course, we believe that the principles and practices within this book may be just the thing to help you change direction.

In the book *Roadmap to Financial Freedom*, by James "Skip" Nichols, we laid out a step-by-step strategic plan useful to anyone who wants to manage their money well, and this book builds upon the first by bringing in the additional experience of Philip Bell and Donna Maddox, who together add over thirty-seven years of financial planning experience, to Skip's five decades of sound financial advice.

It is our goal to help instill confidence and sense of hope for the future of your retirement, to explore the keys to lasting financial independence as well as the factors preventing it, to tackle the challenges facing your retirement, and to help you begin assessing your financial health. We will do all this and more to help answer the pressing questions, "Will my money last?" as well as "Do I have any blind spots?" This process helps you begin to form backup plans so that you can navigate your own successful journey to retirement.

In addition to the nuts and bolts of your finances, however, this book also addresses some of the other practical considerations facing those approaching retirement age. Instead of ones and zeroes, these thought-provoking questions deal with issues we have seen our many clients address, such as, "How will I spend my time?" "Should I move to be nearer my kids?" "What problems might I encounter by moving to a new location?" and "How much money can I afford to loan them if they are experiencing tough times?"

Above we mentioned moving to a new location to be closer to your kids. You might wonder, "How can that cause a problem?" We found many times retirees who move lose the network of friends and relationships that have taken them years to develop.

When Skip's mom moved to be closer to his sister after his dad died, she left behind the network of friends which she and his dad had built over many years. The neighbor she had coffee with several days of the week was gone. The church she attended, which had her favorite discussion group, was gone. In her new location, she had Skip's sisters but she had a very difficult time meeting new friends and establishing new networks. What was to be a move that she would enjoy turned out to be a very lonely time during her last years. Decisions made during retirement are quite important and need to be studied for both the good and the bad that will result from those decisions. Weigh them carefully.

We look at retirement as a new journey, and it is so much more than just entries on a ledger; it is time without having to clock in five days a week, it is time to travel and see things you have wanted to see all your life, and it is time spent with loved ones and doing what you love. Money is what makes many of those things possible, but it is far from everything. Join us as together we look at the roadmap to your retirement.

Chapter 1
Your Dream of Retirement

If you are like most Americans, you have spent the majority of your adult life working. Maybe you started off delivering papers or babysitting, moved up to part time work waiting tables or retail at the mall while going to school, and then entered corporate America where you forged a career. Whether you put most of your time in hourly or for a salary, you have exchanged your time, effort, energy, and focus for a paycheck for decades.

But now something new is on the horizon: a phase of life when your time will become your own and you will harvest the rewards of all that hard work. We call it retirement, and depending on where in your journey you are as you read this book, the thought will likely fill you either with blissful dreams of free time, opportunities, and adventure...or dread as you consider bills, debt, and the unknown.

You will live on what you've accumulated over all those years of working. There will not be a paycheck coming in every two weeks. For many, that is a very uncomfortable feeling and they begin worrying, "Will our money last?" It can also have an impact on their future investment style.

In helping hundreds of clients prepare for retirement, we have learned that most do not have an accurate picture of what they want their retirement to be. Many have dreams, but all too often they lack the experience and tools to make them a reality. Others have fears, but they feel they do not have the tools and resources to address their concerns.

Skip's good friend is an example of someone who did an exceptional job of planning his retirement, and as a result, he has totally enjoyed his experience as a retiree. Let's call him John. John began saving diligently in his company's retirement plan. In his case, it was a 401(k) (his company matched part of his contribution).

John invested the money wisely by setting up a diversified account, which included both stocks and bonds. He did not make the mistake of jumping in and out of the stocks that he owned but stayed invested during both good and bad times. That served him well because when stock prices were down and he made his contribution, he was buying more stocks at cheaper prices so that when the market prices went up he had an extra benefit.

John loved to fly fish, but he realized that it couldn't occupy all of his time. So, during the years before retirement he took oil painting classes, became a relatively knowledgeable person about fine wine, and began working on his golf game. The other day, Skip asked John about how he was enjoying his retirement (it's been three years now since he retired) and he commented, "Skip, I love it, and I think I'm busier now than I've ever been."

Unfortunately, we see many people who didn't plan well for retirement. They didn't save enough money, and they hadn't planned on how they were going to spend all the free time that they would had available. When we visit with them, we can see the boredom on their faces. It's not that they don't enjoy part of retirement, but often they have money worries and they have more time with too few things to do.

But that does not have to be *your* story. In fact, that is why you picked up this book—because we can definitely help with the financial side of retirement planning, and we can encourage you to be like John and to take up new hobbies and invest yourself so that your later years can be the very best ones you've had yet.

Your Dream

Your life has looked like what your day job—typically an 8:00 am to 5:00 pm job—allowed it to be. Your days were busy, your mornings and bedtimes defined by how early you had to be at the office, and your weekends spent trying to catch up on the rest of life. Much of that will change with retirement.

The question now is: "What do you want your retirement to look like?"

It's easy to list off ideas like travel, hobbies, grandchildren, and puttering around the house. But in our experience when the honey-do list is done, the novelty of sleeping in wears off, and you realize your kids have lives that are often structured around their own jobs. Many people struggle to create new lives for themselves. They take a couple trips, maybe spend a little time doing a new hobby, and wrap up the honey-do list.

Within perhaps a year they have established a routine *by default*, and often, it isn't the routine that they would want. Instead of answering the question of what they want their retirement to look like with the same forethought for which they saved for it, they assume they can just figure it out...sometimes with less than rewarding results.

What many people don't realize is that work is not the enemy, and retirement isn't final freedom from that villain. We believe that the Bible is God's Word and can help us in all areas of our lives. We don't believe we've ever read God's Word discussing retirement; therefore, we don't believe we should consider work the villain. Besides giving us that much needed paycheck, our work gives needed structure and shape to our lives, as well as helping us set our routine and more. In all likelihood, that routine and structure has given shape to your life for decades. You are very used to it, and the absence of that routine and structure is going to leave a gaping hole for which few people are truly prepared.

Throughout the course of this book, we are going to help you with specifics—or where to find specifics—about how to handle money, but here at this point in the book, we want to urge you to start this practice with your *dreams*. Just as you will establish specific amounts going into certain funds, and you will set particular sequences of returns and asset allocation, right now we are going to discuss some activities and goals you want for your retirement. These are not the financial goals we will discuss later; these are the dream goals of how you will spend your time. But here is a key of human nature: *the dreams and goals you set for retirement will make all the rest we talk about worth it.*

The company you've worked with has probably done a good job of setting goals each year. Perhaps you've been involved in that process and you've been exposed to the results of setting short and long-term goals, which are normally good.

The college football season just ended recently. At the beginning of the season, the coaches and the players together set out their goals. If goals are important for companies and for sports teams, they certainly aren't going to hurt us. When you have a goal set before you—a dream and vision you're looking forward to—you can do the hard work necessary to attain it. You may have been doing that for years, but now you get to do it for yourself, not your company. A powerful additional benefit is that this will enrich your retirement experience.

Your retirement planning starts now, with setting your goals and defining your dream of retirement. Our feeling is this process should involve you and the important people in your life.

Specify Your Retirement

1. **Do You Have A Vision for Retirement?** Many companies and organizations come together because they get everyone to share a common vision. So, what is most important to you? You may think it is just freedom or travel, but in actual practice, travel itself is likely to take up only a relatively small percentage of your time. You may think it is spending time with your family, but as we mentioned before, your children likely have jobs of their own that take up a lot of their lives.

    Your vision for retirement is about finding out what really matters to you. Your vision is about your desired future.

    A good vision statement reaches for the stars and sets lofty goals; it is about creativity and taking the limits off your thinking, so feel free to color outside the lines. A great example is one long-time friend and client who retired from the Oklahoma Dental College in Oklahoma City. He is studying to receive a master's in medical ethics and plans on teaching part time at the college from which he just retired.

    We have had clients incorporate going back to school and learning about new topics that have interested them in the past.

Others have been involved in working for the general good of their fellow man, their families, or causes. Good vision statements are often brief and are focused on a desirable future. If you're stumped, considered researching how to write a vision statement, and then adapt that to your retirement planning.

Your vision for your retirement may be focused on what kind of person you want to become during retirement. Activities will come and go, but if you seek to clarify who you want to *be*, no matter what you are doing you can come back to this core goal. Do not settle for the easy answer—set a vision for your retirement that you find engaging, sustainable, and not overly dependent on others' schedules.

This is your time—your dream, your vision, and your goals. You have worked hard to get this far, so create a vision that can help begin the rest of your life.

2. **What Is Important About Money to You?** Money doesn't mean the same thing to everyone. For some, it's a necessary evil or a confusing topic. For others, it means freedom to travel, have new experiences, or learn. For others, having money means being able to be generous and improve the lives of others. For others, it means you can have things that perhaps your parents could not afford. Be aware—it may be different for you and your spouse, so it's important to think this through and also to talk it over so you are both clear what is important to you.

    It is also important to then share what's most important to you with your financial advisors. When they understand what motivates you, they will be able to advise you better.

3. **Does Your Retirement Have A Mission?** While a vision statement is about what is important to you and who you want to be during retirement, having a mission can be incredibly focusing (and may change over time). Your mission may define *why* you exist, your objectives in life, and your approach to those objectives.

For instance, if you want to spend more time with your grandchildren, consider *why* you want to do it. Is it just for your own enjoyment? Or is it also to impart something to them? If you want to travel, what are your objectives? Perhaps it is to see the heartland of America, retrace family generations, or see world capitals. Whatever it is, let your mission make you aware of your motivations—your "why."

For decades your job—providing for your family—has helped define your mission in life. You will languish and question your days without a purpose or mission. You don't need a mission in life any less in retirement than any other time of life. We operate best when we have a sense of purpose—even if it is to simply enjoy yourself!

Keep in mind, it's never too late to do some of the things you have wanted to do. The newspaper just featured a story of a grandmother who is eighty-four years old and just got her college degree. What a success story! Our own newsletter recently featured some of Skip's heroes who have done this in retirement.

Life is what you make it, but it probably won't be what you wanted to be…unless you have your plans developed. Keeping your mind and body active may be some of the secrets to a long and productive life. People who put their mind to bed when they retire typically don't enjoy the same length or quality of life as those who stay active.

4. **What Is on Your Bucket List?** We already talked about the honey-do list, which will run out eventually. Try expanding that list to the so-called "bucket list"—things you want to do while you have the energy and resources. While these things can be grand, like kissing your spouse atop the Eiffel Tower in Paris, they can also be intimate, like seeing your grandchildren graduate high school or college. We will plan for these things later in the financial planning session, but for now just let your dreams run wild.

One tip on a good bucket list: involve people you love and make your items *relational*. You will likely never show someone a long check list of bucket items and brag about accomplishing them, but you will always have the memories with loved ones you create while fulfilling these items. That will help give them true lasting worth. A long-time client and friend is named Tom. One of the items on his bucket list was to run a marathon in all fifty states. There's even a group Called the Fifty State Club. Tom not only accomplished his goal after retirement, but he got his son-in-law into marathoning and they ran a marathon in the last twenty states that Tom had to complete to be in the Fifty State club. Tom and his son-in-law have developed memories that will probably be passed on to the next generation—or two. What a wonderful legacy to leave!

5. **What Has Given You Pleasure and Meaning in the Past?** Remember, work is not the enemy. Look back at your work (and personal) life, and see what has given you the most pleasure and sense of meaning and worth. If you felt a swell of pride at accomplishing a difficult task, it is time to start setting challenging tasks for your retirement so you can continue to feel that sense of accomplishment. Just because you are retiring does not mean you should quit challenging yourself! However, where once a boss may have set your challenges, now you get to set them for yourself.

Consider things such as volunteer work, consulting, and mentoring. An acquaintance with whom Skip goes to church is a good example of volunteering for worthy causes. He retired from an oil and gas company and found himself without the daily challenges and involvement of work. After looking around for a while, he decided to help by volunteering for Oklahoma Baptist Foundation. This group of volunteers travel to various locations in and out of the United States that have been devastated by natural disasters. In the last couple years, he has been to Canada to help people who were devastated by the wildfires and spent time in Florida after a recent hurricane.

You have a great deal of experience, wisdom, and skill to offer others, and just because you are no longer using those abilities 8:00-5:00 does not mean that they will not keep providing meaning to you and others during retirement. Make a list of rewarding things that you could do in retirement based on what has given you fulfillment, meaning, and enjoyment in the past. Many of these meaningful activities can take you from the success you had while employed to true significance with your life in retirement.

6. **What Would You Like to Schedule?** Try defining specific periods for activities—so much time for golf or gardening or other activities, so much time with friends, so much time with family, so much time volunteering, and so forth. Develop a schedule you think you would like to keep, and instead of setting one *by default*, be intentional about how you use your time. You can re-evaluate it later to make sure it is realistic and contains all the things you value, but it can be a great help to define this early. Put some detail and structure to your days, and those days will add up into weeks, months, and years of meaningful living.

You do not have to rigidly stick to this schedule, and it may change over time, but if you begin intentionally, you will be able to be more pro-active in those changes. If you use your time by default, it can be hard to break out of that later. Think of it like this: when you get home from dinner and sit down to watch TV, your plan may be to do some exercises or ride the stationary bike while watching. But after sitting down for an hour or so, it's hard to overcome the inertia. Our lives are like this, and inertia works both ways—if you get in the habit of doing healthy, positive behaviors, they are much easier to maintain.

Plan Ahead

People can be tempted to see those specific retirement tips above and think that they will decide those things as they retire. However, in our experience, the people who enjoy their retirement the most are those who have established certain values and then continue to live them out after retirement. For instance, you will have more time for hobbies after retirement, but establishing your interests before you retire gives you known enjoyable activities to do after retirement. In fact, developing specific outside activities before you retire may have an impact on your decision to retire. As a financial planner for over fifty years, you can imagine that Skip has talked with many people who are getting ready to retire or who have already retired. He has encouraged many to expand their activities and goals when, together, they discovered that their activities and plans weren't going to fulfill them. Some decided to continue to work, which is a better alternative than quit a job and feeling bored and unfulfilled only a year after retirement. It can be difficult getting back into an old job with the same income. Further, defining what you value can help you find worthwhile activities like volunteer and consulting opportunities, mentoring relationships, and more *before* you lose the structure of your job.

If you want your life to have purpose and meaning beyond retirement, begin establishing the foundation of those future things while you are still employed. This often simply means recognizing that work is not the only thing that gives you meaning and then making an effort to build up the interests that will carry you into retirement over the next few years.

After a career in IT and technology, Annie was actively contemplating retirement when her husband died unexpectedly. While between their two incomes and his life insurance he had left her well provided for, she knew that she would need to stay busy in retirement. She began volunteer teaching at a technical college, and she volunteered at a local food bank by helping them with their IT needs. Her benefits were immense. She educated, trained, and mentored young people at the college and also provided much-needed support for the local food bank. You can imagine that her life was richer and her sense of self-worth was stronger.

By lining up key activities for much of her week, Annie's transition to retirement was smoother than it otherwise would have been, and she still had satisfying activities contributing to her sense of worth and accomplishment—even during her season of grief. However, because she wasn't required to continue doing any of these things, she was able to do them on her terms and to fill the schedule she designed for herself. Around these things she structured walks three times a week at the gym of her local church to stay in shape, travel domestically and abroad, and a new (to her) Mercedes every few years. She continues to participate in 5K walks and other activities even into her eighties, and when she remarried a few years ago, she introduced her new husband to many of her healthy habits. They now do many of them together.

What do you want your retirement to look like? You would not be reading this book if you did not realize you need a financial plan. Why not plan the rest, as well, like Annie did?

Share Your Dream

For many, retirement is a joint process with a spouse. While one may retire before the other, when you are both retired, both of your lives change dramatically. Most people do not consider the tension and stress that this can put on a marriage, so again you are better off considering the effects of retirement on you both before you get there. The joke between my wife and me is she says, "Honey I married you for better or worse but not for lunch!"

While divorce is less common near retirement than many other ages, couples do well to continue working on their marriages throughout, including in the pre- and retirement years. One of the best pieces of advice we have heard is to *dream together*. When picturing your retirement, do so as a couple.

Creating lists of mutual interests, activities, and bucket list items can be a fun way to plan for the future of retirement. In addition, some of the rewarding things mentioned above, such as volunteer work, can be done together. Activities like this can be a great way to pull you closer and give you common purpose. We always urge couples to find fun activities they both enjoy and to structure their days and weeks around rewarding pursuits that ideally could be done together.

There are some excellent and thoughtful questions for you to talk over together. Among them are questions like these:

- What do you want to do for your children?
- What do you want or need to do for your parents?
- What do you want to do for the world at large?
- Ideally, where would you like to be in ten years?

Unfortunately, we have seen couples who have something like a sudden or forced retirement find that one spouse wants to be active while the other just wants to sit around the house, and the early months and years of this strife can push people toward separate lives. In addition, many hours of sitting around the house, directionless, together can be a strain.

Divorce in these years can be very detrimental to retirement plans, so it is worth your time and energy to work on the health of your marriage with your spouse for many reasons. As a person who has been married for over five decades, Skip is well aware of the work that a marriage needs. At the same time, he knows it is difficult to work on a marriage since we haven't been taught in school or anywhere else how best to keep a marriage strong. We all will benefit at one time or another by having a professional counselor help us with some of the marriage problems we all face. Skip and his wife have been to a number of different counselors at various times in their marriage. Those sessions probably saved their marriage and helped to make it as strong as it is today. There is something special that happens when two people sit down with a counselor. It's like a referee is in the room, and both parties can get things off their chest that otherwise might not be said or heard by the other.

The cost of divorce proceedings is just the beginning, and duplicated household costs for the separated couple mean that retirement savings will dwindle much faster.

If you are planning your retirement or just starting it, get on the same page with your spouse. If you need to sit down with someone like a counselor or pastor to aid that process, it is completely worth the time invested dreaming and building your retirement *together*. You will likely work on your retirement planning with an investment planner, so why would you treat your marriage with any less attention than your finances? Both are very valuable, especially during retirement.

Phillip Bell, CFP®, James K. "Skip" Nichols, ChFC, CLU, Donna Maddox, AIF®

Consulting and Mentoring

When we see work as the enemy, retirement can look like anything *other than work*. However, the truth is that work has often given structure and purpose to your life—just two good things among many. You have likely spent a career developing a certain set of skills or a base of knowledge, and even in today's evolving workforce, those can both still be valuable things. You can use those skills both in a consulting role (where you are not a traditional employee but contract with companies to advise in your field) and/or as a mentor to younger individuals.

In retirement, you can often do the things as a consultant, rather than an employee, and that often means setting your own schedule and (to an extent) your compensation. In addition to staying busy and a feeling of worth, consulting work can help aid or supplement retirement savings. It can be as easy as setting yourself up under your own name "Doing business as" or launching a small LLC to facilitate being an independent contractor.

While it may not return monetary rewards, mentoring can also be highly rewarding. People of the next generations can benefit greatly from your wealth of experience, both inside and outside of your industry. You spent years learning the tools of your trade, the discipline and perspective necessary to use them properly, and likely know your industry inside and out. You can pass along this knowledge, or just the moral fiber it took to get it, to a mentoree in a relationship from which you both will benefit.

Somewhat similar to mentoring and consulting, personal coaching can also utilize your life experience, help others, and contribute financially. Coaching certificates are available from many programs and can almost combine consulting and mentoring.

A notable side benefit to any of these activities is keeping your mind active. Do not discount that like any other part of your body, a mind can atrophy—if you don't use it, you may lose it! Whatever activities you choose, whether they include something like consulting or not, be sure to consider things that will challenge you mentally and help keep you sharp and engaged.

Physical Activity

When retiring, it is important to keep physically active. Some jobs are more physically demanding, and as your body ages your abilities will change. However, we now know that endorphins and other benefits come from exercise—including extending life expectancy and increasing quality of life. If you are not sure what to do, consulting with a personal trainer can help set physical goals, define limitations, or even set up occupational or physical therapy that can restore range of movement or reduce pain.

The goal shouldn't be exercise but *activity*. Exercise sounds like punishment, and who wants to force themselves into some punishing regiment? Activities, though, can be fun and there can be many forms of worthwhile activities that have health benefits. What are you passionate about? For Skip, over the last fifteen years fly fishing has become a very important part of his life. Whether catching fish or not, it takes him to some of the most beautiful spots in nature here in Oklahoma, Colorado, Arkansas, or Montana.

For you, perhaps it's walking, which may be sprinkled in many different parts of our beautiful cities or states. Maybe you want to take up pickle ball or tennis or kayaking. The point is, there are innumerable things that are fun to do and great for keeping your body and mind healthy.

Many people want to jump straight into activities like golf or tennis after retirement—but they have not exercised regularly. This can be a recipe for injury. According to researchers, even individuals in their 80s and 90s can restore flexibility, endurance, and strength with a moderate exercise plan.[1] The list of benefits to regular exercise don't stop just because you are retired—from reducing medication to decreased risk of early death to weight control, they are all still very valid (sometimes even more so) in retirement. According to some studies, retirees with active lifestyles who

---

[1] https://www.usatoday.com/story/money/personalfinance/2014/01/19/retirees-exercise-physical-activity/4262151/

exercise moderately also show less deterioration of the brain's white matter, which is liked to decision making and other brain functions.[2] So what is good for your body is also good for your mind.

To motivate yourself to exercise, experts recommend setting activity goals such as completing a 5k (a five-kilometer walk is about three miles), then breaking that goal into bites of 20-30 minutes of exercise multiple times a week until you reach it. Then create new, more challenging goals. Also, experts suggest finding others in your same situation—i.e. other retirees seeking to stay active. Some health clubs, gyms, and even some local churches can help with this.

Location and Travel

Some people dream of relocating after retirement, and this can be a great reward for a lifetime of work. Places with nice climate can be very popular retirement destinations. However, few people consider the adjustment periods involved with relocating. From finding new places to shop to locations for medical care, relocating isn't something to be done lightly. Like everything else we have suggested in this chapter, we advocate doing your homework.

Some want to relocate to be nearer to children and grandchildren. Again, the same concerns are valid. While you probably want to spend more time with your grandchildren, you likely do not want to become *just* the de facto babysitter, no matter how much fun that may be for a time. Before diving into a relocation based on being near kids, try traveling to see them and the places you may consider relocating to find out what you really like about your new location. You definitely do not want to go to the expense to relocate…only to find that in a short time you are unhappy and want to relocate again. Our suggestion, from years of working with clients who were entering retirement, is to temporarily relocate to that area perhaps for a month or two. It will cost a little money while you're staying temporarily in a motel, but this gives you an opportunity to see all the advantages and disadvantages that location

---

[2] http://time.com/5162477/exercise-risk-dementia/

has. Ask yourself questions like these: What are the citizens like? Do you like the weather in the good and bad times of the year? Do you miss your friends and associates from back home? Was it just fascination about this new place, or is it really where you want to spend the rest your life?

The advantages to staying put and simply traveling include preserving your social network and the infrastructure you are familiar with. We can take our social network and infrastructure for granted, but it is a very important part of our life. Uprooting ourselves may be much more traumatic than we could imagine. It is incredibly important to have a robust network of friends and companions when you retire, because all the social interaction from your workplace will disappear; you'll want to spend time with people, so established friends can be vital. Similarly, just navigating a new place, or trying to find important places like restaurants and medical facilities, can be a challenge. It may be something as simple as the food that turns you off. When Skip first moved to Louisiana, his parents had trouble getting used to the Cajun way of cooking

We have talked a little bit about travel, saying that your overall travel time after retirement may not be as high as you first think. In our financial planning, we always help couples define a travel budget and anticipate how much travel they actually want to do after retiring.

Obviously, we want to figure out the financial details of traveling, but it is also important to consider your physical abilities while considering travel. One couple we worked with really wanted to travel in an RV to see the country and to camp, but they neglected to consider that one of them sometimes needed a wheelchair! They may exist, but we have yet to see a wheelchair-accessible RV, and we knew they may not want to try going into the woods even if they could get there. Instead, we recommended this couple consider a certain number of larger trips each year to places with good handicap accessibility and activities that they could both do.

Phillip Bell, CFP®, James K. "Skip" Nichols, ChFC, CLU, Donna Maddox, AIF®

Live Your Dream

As financial planners, it is our goal to help our clients live the dream of their retirement. From where they live to how much their living expenses will cost, from travel to volunteer or consulting work, we try to create sound financial plans that anticipate needs, wants, and even the unexpected.

We have found that there are some major keys to financial independence that have helped our clients live out those dreams. In the next chapter, we are going to share some of these secrets with you. Whether you are a savvy investor looking to take your retirement planning to the next step or you are just getting started, we have put some of the biggest keys to your financial future together into one place, and we think you'll like the results of implementing these secrets to financial success. These are powerful proven methods that you can adopt and increase you potential for success in retirement. Two of the most important are the basic power of compound interest and how the Rule of 72 can revolutionize your investment strategy.

Chapter 2

The Keys to Your Financial Independence

It is our hope that the previous chapter was food for thought and inspired you to give definition to your dreams of retirement. With a dream in mind and goals that go beyond more zeroes and dollar signs, you will set yourself up for a hopeful future. When you can visualize it, you will have an easier time taking the steps to get there.

In this chapter we are going to talk about some of those steps—**keys to financial independence** that will help you understand the tools and principles of building retirement savings. If you already have a very keen financial grasp, these things will be helpful reminders; and if you are just beginning your journey toward retirement savings, these keys may be some of the most important concepts we can teach you.

It is our desire that you are able to enjoy your retirement. When you are aware and planning for things like taking advantage of the power of compound interest, inevitable market volatility, gradual inflation, increased life expectancy, and more, you position yourself for success. We will talk about the issues that can prevent financial success and the challenges to retirement in the following chapters, but in this chapter we want to help you understand some things you can use to your favor:

1. Understanding the Power of Compound Interest & The Rule of 72
2. Doing the Right Thing
3. Staying on the Train
4. Coming to Terms with Behavioral Finance
5. Using "Out of Sight Out of Mind"

6. Having a Plan B
7. Getting Financial Help.

Understand the Power of Compound Interest & The Rule of 72

Compound interest[3] is calculated not just on the money you initially invest (the principal), but also the accumulated interest that money generates over time. It is possibly the single most powerful force in finance—for better or for worse. We educate our clients about this principle and how it works, and then we move on to a related concept called The Rule of 72 that has direct application on your retirement savings.

The Rule of 72 is a powerful concept for any investor to catch. It isn't terribly complicated, but it can completely change the way you look at your retirement planning when you understand this well-proven concept.

The Rule of 72 is a financial principle that says that if you divide the interest rate you are receiving on an investment into the number 72, it will tell you the number of years for a lump sum of money to double. (You can visit our website, F-P-R.com, for a more complete explanation of The Rule of 72[4] if you would like more info.) A retirement account with a small rate of return (say 3%) will take a great deal longer to double your money than an account with a higher rate of return (say 12%), but the questions we get are things such as, "Is 12% possible?" and "What about risk?" So, let's look at some examples to see how this plays out.

Let's say John invested $5,000 in a conservative fund. At 3%, his money will double (ie, 72/3 = 24 years) in 24 years. If John put a lump sum in at age 40, his money would have doubled by age 64 to $10,000.

Sherri took a different route and invested in a fund that averaged 12% (we use these percentages of return for a reason, which we'll get

---

[3] https://www.investopedia.com/terms/c/compoundinterest.asp
[4] https://www.investopedia.com/terms/c/compoundinterest.asp
https://www.usatoday.com/story/money/personalfinance/2015/04/25/adviceiq-doubling-your-money/26339307/

to later). Her money will double in only six years—a huge difference! (72/12=6 years).

$5,000 @ 12% 6 years 12 years 18 years 24 years
$10,000 $20,000 $40,000 $80,000

Let's say that Sherri is able to invest the same $5,000 initially at age 40—and *she leaves it in*, which is incredibly important. According to The Rule of 72, in six years, Sherri's money should have doubled to $10,000. After 12 years, she has $20,000, after 18 years she has $40,000, and after 24 years Sherri will have $80,000 compared to John's $10,000.

The question we ask our clients is this: who is *safer*, John or Sherri?

The typical answer is often John and his stable 3%, but in most cases we would argue that Sherri is actually "safer" because the person with the most money at age sixty-four is "safer." (We will get into risk management in another portion of the book, but we want to emphasize the power of The Rule of 72 here to make a point.)

Now, this may all sound too fantastic to be true, and many people ask if it is realistic to expect any investment to average 12% over the course of 24 years. In fact, many people will tell you that it is impossible. And that is where, during a session with a client, we pull out a fund from American Funds that has been around for over *80 years*. During that time, it has indeed averaged 12%, and we show them the history of the fund to see if The Rule of 72 would work using this fund. Starting in 1934, we look to see what a one-time $10,000 investment would return if the investor had stayed the course. Even accounting for market downturns and bad years, including severe recessions, The Rule of 72 proves true—even for this supposedly more volatile, risky fund—and in most periods of six years indeed would double the investment.

This is the power of compound interest!

You are not going to retire on $80,000, and we do not recommend our clients put all their investment dollars into a single mutual fund, but we do this to illustrate the point that compound interest is an

Phillip Bell, CFP®, James K. "Skip" Nichols, ChFC, CLU, Donna Maddox, AIF®

incredibly potent tool for your retirement planning. Not only does it help increase your investment, it increases your *options*. One reason we would argue that Sherri is in fact "safer" than John is that her additional money presents her with additional options.

We will get into some of the prerequisites for making a strategy that includes investing in a fund like this shortly, and in another chapter we will look at the allocation of funds. But for now, the most important thing to do is to note that Sherri's fund *averaged* 12% over the course of time. In other words, some years it was up and other years it was down. It was vital that Sherri did not panic during periods where the fund under-performed and she "*stayed on the train,*" as we like to say. Market fluctuations, including recessions, are *going* to happen. In fact, we expect them. But we know from over 80 years of history that Sherri's fund, over the course of 26 years, is going to average its 12% for her—if she stays the course. With inflation muted today, a 10% return could be more realistic. Either way, the power of compound interest remains.

From a financial security point of view, the more you can get your money to double, the better! Which would you rather have? Ten thousand dollars after 24 years or $80,000? Which would give you more flexibility and financial safety? The compounding effect is what makes interest so powerful.

This is especially important when we consider, as we will discuss in more detail in chapter four, that your investments need to outpace inflation. We expect inflation to average around 2.5%, so John's investments are *barely* outstripping inflation. He may have more money after 24 years than he started with, but his money will be worth less. Inflation works the same way as compound interest, only it works to your detriment, and you must form a sound financial plan that accounts for it.

When people grasp the power of compound interest, it emphasizes how important it is to stay in it for the long haul (which we call staying on the train). The important thing is not to look at the amount invested; it's actually to look at the percentage of return. This is the best way to make use of the power of compound interest and The Rule of 72. However, you will best be able to utilize the power of compound interest if you are doing the right things and have money to invest in the first place, so let's look at four key principles for financial independence.

> Note: The rule of 72 is a mathematical concept and does not guarantee investment results nor functions as a predictor of how an investment will perform. It is an approximation of the impact of a targeted rate of return. Investments are subject to fluctuating returns and there is no assurance that any investment will double in value.

Doing the Right Things

In the next chapter, we are going to talk in detail about four things we feel sabotage financial independence. But before we point out what *not* to do, we want to take some time to look at four things that we feel historically contribute to our financial independence and well-being. In fact, we can point out that failing to follow these principles has cost America greatly in recent decades and that these old-fashioned values represent the surest path back to financial wellness for individuals and our country. We simply call them **Doing the Right Things**, and they are as follows: Spend Less Than You Make, Have Cash Available, Avoid Excessive Debt, and Take A Long-Term Perspective.

1. **Spend Less Than You Make**—This is arguably the most basic key to financial independence. It's so simple, yet it seems so hard for people in today's economy to do! We live in a world where credit is readily available, where interest rates have been low for an extended period of time, and where society itself emphasizes instant gratification and ignoring the consequences. Constant marketing urges us to go, to buy, and to enjoy— *NOW!* It makes feeling and instant gratification king! These things constitute a terrible investment strategy, and they are directly responsible for the excessive burdens of debt, failed mortgages, and poor national economic habits that are hurting individuals, families, and even entire states and countries! If we could all simply abide by this single principle, we could

ignore everything else and still be far more assured of financial success. But it does not end with your retirement; it's a lifelong principle that will dictate your distribution strategy in retirement. Properly managed, this principle can see you through your entire life—retirement years included. We need to make sure we teach our kids to spend less than you make!

2. **Have Adequate Cash Available**—It isn't enough to just spend less than you make. You have to expect the unexpected and plan ahead for things. For instance, smart businesses know that certain costs are inevitable, even if you do not know exactly when they will happen. Underwriters can tell you how often, on average, a roof needs to be replaced, and a good accountant can help make sure a business has planned ahead for the day when the building needs a new roof. The same is true for your home—you can plan ahead even for unexpected expenses, such as a storm damaging your roof, and instead of being caught flat-footed, you can be ready for the unexpected (at least financially). Similarly, things like Christmas are not emergencies—it comes around every year, and you buy presents for family and friends each year. Instead of being surprised or caught without necessary cash, you can plan ahead for such things and have cash available for those things. This is also true for opportunities…

3. **Avoid Unnecessary Debt**—Debt itself isn't bad. Unnecessary or uncontrolled or excessive debt, however, is a bad thing. It can easily get away from you, and it is the power of compound interest *turned against you.* If you do not have cash available, you will wrack up unnecessary debt. When the storm damages the roof and you have to come up with your deductible, or when Christmas rolls around and you want to buy the kids presents, without cash available you will resort, all too often, to adding debt. Borrowing money to buy your house or car or certain other things can be wise; giving your money away and paying the penalty of compound interest to the credit card company, however, is not wise. It will cost you, and every year you spend in excessive, unnecessary debt siphons money away from funds you could be investing in your retirement plan.

4. **Take A Long-Term Perspective**—You may be familiar with the book "Good to Great." A long-term perspective means you might delay something "good" (buying something on your credit card just because it caught your eye) for something "great" (staying on the train and keeping your focus on saving and investing). You will delay short-term gratification so that you can enjoy your retirement more in the long run. The Rule of 72 requires a long-term perspective and staying on the train. You have to stick with it; if you bailed out after a few years or come and go too often, you could potentially lose all the benefits of your investment portfolio's returns. Wisdom tells us to avoid quick gains—because they can go just as quickly as they come! Being patient and letting your money (and compound interest) work for you is often the most assured path to financial independence.

Stay on the Train

We call the long-term approach staying on the train. If you own equities, they are going to go down sometimes. Focus on the fact you do not own the stock market; instead you own great American companies. These companies produce products we use every day of our lives. They make money, pay dividends, and over time go up in value because of the products people around the world buy from them. In the example above where Sherri averaged a 12% return on her investment, she did not do so each year. In fact, she didn't average that even every two or three years on a number of occasions. Most periods of six years, however, she would have doubled her money—and in some periods, more than that. Sherri had to take a long-term view of her investments such as the 24 years in our example.

However, if she would have hopped in and out of the mutual fund, trying to "work the market," she *definitely would not* have enjoyed that 12% return!

One client, whom we'll just call Betty, worked for a national grocery chain in an office job. She never made a great deal of money in any given year, but she methodically put money into her company's 401(k) plan, lived below her means, and took a long-term approach.

Phillip Bell, CFP®, James K. "Skip" Nichols, ChFC, CLU, Donna Maddox, AIF®

Over the course of time, we watched this hard-working woman save up over a million dollars—all of which was working for her with the power of compound interest. As of this writing, Betty has been retired 12 years...and thanks to following these principles, her accounts have actually *grown* since she retired even though she is withdrawing from her investment monthly! Betty lives comfortably and enjoys her home, activities, and friends and family—without the concern of running out of money. Betty embodied these keys of financial independence, and even though she didn't make a great deal, she used it wisely to prepare a comfortable retirement.

Come to Terms with Behavioral Finance (Greed and Fear)

Few people know this, but our brains are actually hard-wired to make *bad* financial decisions! We naturally make assumptions without good evidence, we see correlations where there are none, and we can fall victim to a herd mentality. Emotional financial decision making usually results in poor decisions, and whenever we deviate from proven logic, it tends to have poor long-term results. Understanding this involves the study of Behavioral Finance.[5]

Men and women may have trouble in any of these areas; they are no respecter of person or gender. Men, however, frequently think of themselves as unemotional decision-makers, when in fact they are just as likely as anyone to make decisions this way. This can create a blind spot. Interestingly, we have seen that women can be better investors because they communicate more openly with their circle about what is and is not working with their investments, whereas sometimes men can tend to be more competitive. We have seen that emotional decision-makers can overcome their knee-jerk responses, get education, learn what works, and make intelligent, logical, and informed decisions. But whatever your gender, personality, or background, our desire is that this book will help you with your financial decisions!

---

[5] https://www.investopedia.com/university/behavioral_finance/

You have heard it said that "opposites attract." This is also often true financially. Typically, one person fits the model of a "saver" while the other is often a "spender." One is often more conservative, and the other is more of a risk-taker. Some couples are used to being told that makes one "good" at finances and the other "bad," but in fact we typically need both. The conservative saver is tempted to take the route that seems safe and risk free and needs the risk-taker to balance them with higher-yield investments. Similarly, the spender may, by themselves, tend to over-draw accounts, while the saver reigns in those spending habits to keep to the budget. Neither is "wrong," and often couples need one another's balance and perspective. We always suggest our clients discover which one is which (if they don't already know) so they can be more comfortable acknowledging their strengths and weaknesses.

These things and many others are involved in actively *fighting* poor decision making, and one of the easiest ways to do this is simply to keep our investments Out of Sight, Out of Mind. If you are not looking at it constantly and not tempted to make changes to your accounts, you are less likely to make a poor decision—it can be as simple as that.

Using "Out of Sight, Out of Mind"

The principle we call Out of Sight, Out of Mind has incredible power. It's the idea that if you leave it alone, you will do better than if you try to micro-manage your investments. In fact, the people who tell us something like, "I don't know what's in my 401(k)" are frequently more successful.

The key is to let the compound interest do its work and the market work for you long-term. Occasionally reviewing your portfolio, and making wise decisions, is important, but we frequently tell people *not* to look at their investments every day or even every month. (This assumes you have a diversified portfolio comprised of stock in great companies and solid bonds.)

The market will fluctuate. If you are watching it like a hawk, your temptation will be to take your money out and move it around, occurring fees, penalties, and the natural consequence of human behavior.

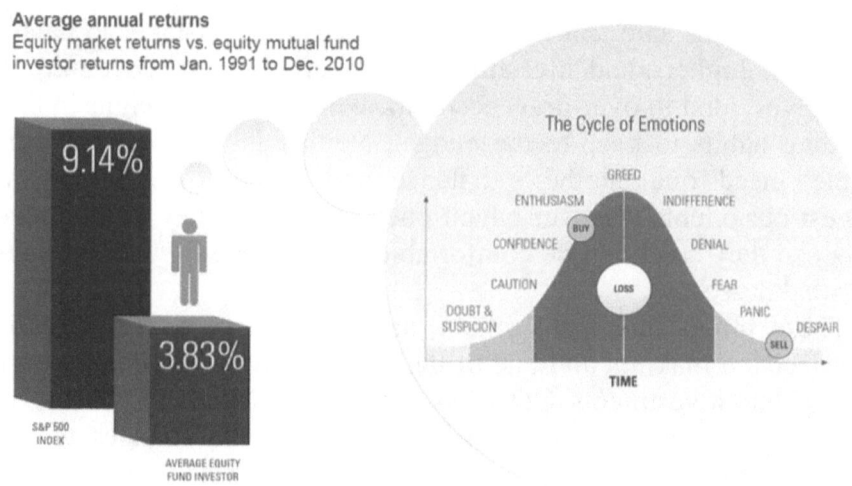

As shown, the average equity fund investor captured only a small part of the market return over the 20 years ending 2010. It is tempting to make emotional decisions, especially when markets are volatile. This can lead to buying when prices are high and selling when prices are low.

After the financial crisis of 2008 and 2009, when prices were low, it took years before people had the confidence to buy back in. They missed the lowest prices, and they waited to see that things looked better before they got back in. Then, they bought and bought as prices rose. Had they stayed with it and ridden out the storm, they would have been so much better positioned to take advantage of the low prices after the drop. You want to buy in when things are low, but what assurances do we have that things won't get worse? If you're trying to time the market, you don't know when things are going to get better or worse. If you stay in, you are ready to ride the recovery.

We also like to impress upon our clients that the amount of money isn't the focus; the percentage of return should be. One client was a blue-collar machinist, and he had saved up over $400,000 over time through hard work and careful savings. He saw it increase $20,000 in one year, which was about half of his yearly salary and to him seemed like a large increase. However, that was only a 5% gain. If it later dropped that amount, he feels the pain of a $20,000 loss and thinks, "I could've bought a car for that."

If he takes his money out and moves it around, he may never see the fruits of his patience. If you don't look at it too frequently, you will not have the temptation toward the negative thoughts and worries of the moment. The machinist needed to stay on the train and ride out the low point. If he'd do so, he would typically see the market recover his lost money and give him the higher percentage yield he needed to make real progress.

Have a Plan B

Hope is *not* an investment strategy. Hope is a good thing, but if you are trusting hope that your retirement plans can handle changes in the economy or you hope that you can sustain excessive withdrawals, that "hope" is ill-founded.

We know historically since WWII that our economy has experienced a bear market recession—a market drop of 20% or more that is sustained over a period of time—roughly every five to six years. There are of course exceptions to this average—during the writing of this the current bull market has lasted longer than that average period of time—but it is important to accept that market fluctuations are going to happen. It is not a matter of "if" but "when."

However, this is not a cause for fear, only sound planning. In essence, the actions you take with your investment or retirement strategy change to match the times, and if you are currently planning for retirement during a bear market, you want to account for these market fluctuations—and what to do when one hits—in your planning.

Phillip Bell, CFP®, James K. "Skip" Nichols, ChFC, CLU, Donna Maddox, AIF®

If you retire at age sixty-five and life expectancy has you living into your nineties, history tells us you may experience five or six recessions. For us as financial planners, this means that we want to build this eventuality into our retirement plans and strategies—and then encourage you to stick with them. We can run advanced financial projections to see if your retirement plan is "recession proof," but the reality is that much of weathering these economic downturns comes back to how *you* execute your retirement plan.

We have seen that having an active withdrawal strategy is vitally important, especially in the down years. Having a good strategy for the bad years can be more important than growth in the good years.

Remember, if you are not micro-managing your accounts, you will tend to avoid poor decisions. However, how you handle the various "buckets" that hold your retirement funds will need to change from one market condition to the other. But whether you are operating on Plan A or Plan B, a great deal of successfully handling these challenges comes down to your discipline in sticking with your plan and budget. Periodic reviews with your financial planner can help you stay on course.

It's no good to have a plan…if you do not follow it.

Over-withdrawal (or no distribution strategy) is typically the biggest problem we see as financial advisors. Perhaps there were unexpected expenses, a child needed some financial support, or a couple traveled more than anticipated; any of these things can draw more money than planned out of your various buckets. Sometimes we find ourselves just doing things in a more extravagant way than anticipated.

For instance, one client found that he was running out of money more quickly than anticipated, and when we got to the bottom of it, we found that he was eating out at nicer restaurants much more often than expected. With lunch and dinner at nicer restaurants costing more than it has in past years (and he was eating out most of the days in the week), he was literally eating through his retirement at an unexpected rate! While this alone was not the only factor, it was a leading cause of increased daily expenses, and a partial recipe for change was simple—he decided to eat at home more! That alone perhaps oversimplifies it, but when the numbers added up, this was a significant extra expense that contributed to a trend of over withdrawal. Another couple were trading their cars out every three years instead of their original plan to keep them for seven to ten years; it can all add up.

At the start of retirement, it may be tempting to see the large pool of assets you have worked so hard to accumulate as seemingly inexhaustible. Compared to what you made in a month or even a year, it may seem like a great deal of money. And, with some discipline and forethought, it can last; however, if you draw it out faster than planned, it may not. And the amount that can be drawn may be different in one market than another, which is why it is important to sit down with your financial advisor for periodic reviews, or what we like to call "strategy sessions."

Team Up with A Good Financial Advisor

Even the best athletes have a coach; they don't get on the court or take to the field without strategy, planning, and support. And just as a good coach can help keep a team on track, a good financial advisor can help you in a wide variety of ways. We know that our clients often simply need a little advice and coaching to do the right things they already know to do. We just encourage them to take those right next steps.

We will cover details on how to pick a financial advisor in chapter 9, but as a key to financial independence, picking a good financial advisor to help you is very important. Perhaps the biggest service we provide our clients is one of offering *perspective*. Our respective years of experience is compounded by helping numerous clients, each one of whom has a different story and different experience as the market shifts over time. We have seen so many stories play out, a good financial advisor can offer you perspective on your current situation.

Often, helping pick investments is only a small portion of what a financial advisor does. "Money" has many moving pieces, and helping clients reconsider poor decisions, seeing the big picture, and understanding client's long-term goals are all major ways a financial advisor adds value to your retirement plans.

In many cases, an initial consultation is free, but the services—such as advanced investment modeling—we provide can make the difference between a retirement that wavers with market changes or one that is built to achieve your objectives even during economic downturns or recessions. A good line of open communication is vital to taking advantage of all that your financial advisor has to offer.

Now that we have covered some of the keys of financial success, we want to spend the next chapter talking about issues that will prevent or hinder your financial success. We are not going to talk about excessive debt, picking the "wrong" mutual fund, or market fluctuations. Instead, we want to talk about how fear, greed, selfishness, and noise can affect your thinking and sabotage your retirement.

Chapter 3
Traps that Prevent Financial Independence

Just as there are keys to financial independence, there are traps that prevent it. Before you start thinking about problems like debt or withdrawing too much from your account, we want to again address some of the underlying principles. In our consulting, we have seen four things more than anything else that derail retirement plans—sometimes before they even start. These are not simply financial traps, these are *life traps*, and when you avoid them, you set yourself up not just for success financially but in many other areas of life.

The four biggest traps that prevent financial success are as follows:

1. Fear
2. Greed
3. Selfishness
4. Noise

These may not be the traps you were expecting, but we guarantee that these underlying factors will sabotage your efforts if left unchecked. Let's look at them each together—and perhaps more importantly, let's see how to address and overcome each.

Fear

Fear is arguably the biggest reason people sell low and buy high. It leads us, as we touched on in the last chapter, to make poor financial choices based on emotion, not logic. When we are afraid, we are not thinking clearly and logically, and we are even more prone to poor financial decisions.

Phillip Bell, CFP®, James K. "Skip" Nichols, ChFC, CLU, Donna Maddox, AIF®

We will reference the Dalbar Study multiple times in this book because is an incredibly instructive look into the way emotions (fear and greed prime among them) impact our investing. According to the study, a ten-year period of equity market returns from the S&P 500 Index showed a rate of return of 9.14%. However, the average equity fund investor, during that same time, showed a return of 3.3%. Why?

Simply put, fear and other emotions inspire us to make poor financial decisions, as we stated earlier. It spooks us into selling low (fear) and buying high (greed). The study shows a chart of the "Cycle of Emotions"—the roller coaster bell curve that negates the benefits of the market and limits the returns of emotional investors.

We tend to feel doubt and suspicion when stocks are low, which gives way to caution and later to confidence. During this time, the stock prices are rising. As we enter into a period of enthusiasm, we tend to buy. Greed sets in, and we buy more because stocks continue to grow in value. The market inevitably fluctuates, and the value of those stocks begin to drop. At first, we tend to be indifferent. Then denial sets in, followed by fear and later panic. At this point, many people sell as their emotions take them into despair—and we have bought when the stocks were high, and we have sold them when they are low. Any gains are often lost, and we have ridden the emotional roller coaster to little or no gains, and often to loss.

Market timing and fluctuations are a large reason for people's fear. They distrust the market because their image of stocks and investing is actually more accurately a description of gambling motivated by greed and hamstrung by fear. This is not true investing.

These emotional traps and the pitfalls, loss, and stress that come with them are *not* part of the life of a sound, savvy investor, and they are opposite the rational wisdom a good financial advisor will share with you. You do not need to fear the market's inevitable fluctuations when you have adequately planned ahead.

We meet fear with education and sound planning. We will not even *have* a great deal of fear when we understand that these fluctuations are normal and common and we stay on the train and let compound interest from a diversified portfolio do its work for us.

Greed

Most people do not see themselves as being "greedy." We are not talking about being a stingy, green-eyed monster here. When we talk about "greed," we are talking about the temptation to try to take shortcuts and work the system (which amounts to gambling) instead of letting the system work for you over time.

Greed lures people into chasing after quick growth opportunities at the expense of wise investment practices. It inspires people to become gamblers in the market, not investors, and it leaves them pursuing the next big thing and hoping for a big payday instead of patiently letting the market, compound interest, and The Rule of 72 do their work.

The problem is, when we go after the high fliers...we're often betting on last year's winners that have already peaked and are likely coming back down to earth.

For example, in the late 90s the Tech bubble was swelling. People were making incredible amounts of money, and greed tempted many to take their money out of diversified retirement accounts and put it all into tech stocks. They heard that someone was making more money than they were, and they chased those incredible results for themselves...

Right in time for the Tech Bubble to pop in 2000. Trying to chase yesterday's high fliers often results in getting in when those stocks are at their height (buying high) and then watching them come back down again, only to panic when the bottom drops out (selling low).

Who knew that March of 2009 would be the bottom of the market? If someone had invested in 2007, they would have seen the market peak—and then begin to drop. In 2008, investors probably got concerned, and by 2009 many would be in a full-blown panic! However, those who went to cash at that point would have missed out on some of the most amazing growth the market has ever experienced. By 2012, any losses experienced in 2009 would be recouped, yet many got out at the low point and potentially missed the recovery.

When you bail out of your carefully ordered, diversified portfolio to chase the high fliers, it is risky, and it is just a form of greed. It may work for a time, but eventually you will guess wrong, wait too long, or something else will happen, and that gambled money will get lost and be difficult to recover. Whereas if you stay on the train and let compound interest work for you, your intelligently planned portfolio will weather downturns and help your retirement savings continue to build or provide your necessary income.

The four most dangerous words in investing, according to John Templeton: *"It's different this time."* It's tempting to think that it will be different this time because we've never had the industries we have today—incredible advances in technology and other sectors that seem (for a while) to break the rules, as the Tech Bubble did.

If we do not know (and learn from) the past, we are doomed to repeat it. Instead of gambling away retirement funds due to greed, we urge the patient, long-term "stay on the train" approach and we discussed in the previous chapter. Those keys to financial independence will help combat the temptation to give in to greed.

Selfishness

It may seem slightly counter-intuitive, but selfishness can actually be a trap that prevents our financial independence. We talked about the role of fear and greed, and selfishness could be considered applying those concepts over time. If fear incites us to sell low and greed invites us to buy high, selfishness is what urges us to think of only today. It urges us to take too much out too quickly and to spend it only on ourselves.

Now, we are not saying that you should selflessly use your retirement savings to everyone else's benefit. Think of it like this: when the flight attendant demonstrates when to put on the oxygen mask if the cabin should lose pressure on a flight, they always tell parents to put on their own mask before helping their children. Why? Is it selfishness? No—they know that you cannot help others if you are not in a strong position yourself.

We will talk later about how to determine if you have the resources to give money to those in need, such as helping a child through a painful and expensive divorce, but here we simply want to establish that it is not selfish to account for your own provision throughout decades of retirement. Nor is it selfish to know how much you need to live on.

However, the lure of over-drawing on your principal to buy things or live an unsustainable lifestyle can be a draw when you see all the amounts you have earned totaled in one place. It can be tempting to want to spend it and have fun…at the long-term expense of your retirement accounts. This is selfishness.

Instead, we urge retirees to use the same logical methods for your distribution strategy as you have used to accumulate your funds. When you do this, and when you live within your means, invest wisely, and take a long-term approach, you can have not only money for yourselves but also to leave as an inheritance.

Noise

We are bombarded with more information today than any time ever in the history of humanity. It has been said that we are exposed to as much information *in a single day* as those in the 15th century would have seen in a *lifetime*. And more information is being generated at a geometric rate.

Not only is more being created, we have unprecedented access to it. Smart phones and smart watches have added new sources to the list that once more limited to computers and, if you go even further back, newspapers.

We call this invasion of data "noise" or "clutter." It is quite simply *information overload*. In keeping with this, data about what the markets are doing is now readily available at any hour, night and day, as close to you as your phone or even your wrist.

This noise can make it very hard to stay on the train because it tempts us to think we've made incorrect decisions (fear) or that we could be doing better if our money were elsewhere (greed).

The noise isn't just data, however—if it were, we might be OK. Part of the problem is that news sources have shifted from reporting the news factually and impartially to seeking ratings and readers. Attention comes from sensationalism, and so the constant drive is to *create* news—to create something that will grab your precious attention for a brief moment away from the overload of data bombarding your senses. This commonly manifests itself in eye-catching, sensational, and *negative* headlines meant to draw your eye and inspire fear or greed.

We must limit the noise. You will always be second-guessing yourself if you are watching every detail of the market like a hawk and sucking up the titillating details that the news media puts out to tempt you to look. You will rarely feel comfortable with your decisions, and you will wish that your portfolio was doing just a little bit better...

As we have said before, the best investors we typically see are the ones who paid little of this kind of attention to their investments. They do their due diligence, they do periodic reviews with us, and they make intelligent adjustments to fit market conditions. However, they are not hanging on their phone and watching their favorite pet stocks climb or crash. They have chosen a different value system, one that encourages the long game, patience, and logic over sensational get-rich-quick schemes, trying to chase the high fliers, and emotional investing.

Our best advice to you on this—limit the noise. Only check on things periodically, and do not let yourself get suckered into sensationalist headlines of greed or fear.

Now that we have looked at some of the underlying concepts that can prevent your financial independence, in the next chapter we're going to look at the specific nuts-and-bolts challenges of retirement. From specific difficulties that we know to expect to the unexpected that we nevertheless must plan for, these problems are the hurdles you must overcome. Join us as we help you learn to handle these challenges.

Chapter 4
Overcoming the Challenges of Retirement

We spent the last chapter talking about the traps of fear, greed, selfishness, and noise. These are underlying problems that can subvert your thinking and prevent you from making (and sticking to) a logical retirement plan. In this chapter, we are going to examine some of specific challenges facing people entering retirement—and how to overcome them.

In This Life You Will Face Trials

It has been joked that death and taxes are the only two constants of life, but in reality, you should also expect certain challenges to retirement such as inflation and market fluctuations. Let's briefly explore some of the known difficulties you will see during your retirement years. Another trial is excess withdrawals, and asset allocation…which should be two additional areas to discuss

1. Inflation—Inflation means that the money you save today will be worth *less* in 30 years than it is today. If you were to put all of your retirement funds in your mattress and did not touch them for decades, your money would be able to do less with each passing year. Yes, it would be safe, but it would not go as far. Similarly, accounts that generate a low return may not outpace inflation and could be the equivalent of keeping your money in your mattress at home.

    We estimate inflation to rise at about 2.5% for the financial projections we do with our clients, but some studies have shown we have experienced an average rate of inflation of

3.8% since the creation of the Federal Reserve. At the writing of this book, we live in a low inflationary environment with a core inflation of about 1.9%. In other decades, such as the 70s, inflation spiked at 15-16%, has lingered at 7%, and has been even lower than today, but generally the Fed tries to monitor factors such as wage inflation and to balance inflation with economic growth. If they sense inflation is increasing more quickly than they want it to be, they will raise interest rates to help reign it in.

While inflation is low today, it may not stay that way, and we want to shield retirements from rising inflation that could occur in decades to come. We want people to understand what that would do to the spending power of their money, but also how it necessitates that their investments' returns outpace inflation just to keep them from *losing* spending power.

Donna shares the example with clients of how her childhood home in Colorado was once $18,000 when her parents purchased it. That same house is worth $420,000 at the writing of this book. Imagine if her parents wanted to buy the same house today that they had bought years ago…using funds they had set aside then. While real estate has not appreciated in all areas as much it has in Colorado, this is just one of many factors that contribute to inflation. When her parents retired in the 70s, their electric bill was $30 a month; today, it might be $150. Wages have increased to match, and all rolled together it forces up inflation one factor at a time.

Your retirement planning must accept that inflation *will* happen and account for it as effectively as possible. When learning about risk acceptance and the desired yield from your investments, it is vital that you consider your investments' ability to outstrip inflation and translate that understanding into the actual dollar amounts involved so that your retirement can still be comfortable in two or three decades.

We start our financial planning by calculating what it costs in today's dollars for you to live comfortably. Understanding that it will cost between 75-100% of your current income to maintain your standard of living, we then project that number times 2.5% in order to determine what you will need to drawing out in in future years. This kind of modeling and inflation-proofing your retirement is one of the biggest services a good financial advisor can help with, and when done properly it can set your mind at ease knowing you have accounted for the challenge of inflation.

2. <u>Rising Health Care Costs</u>—We expect health care costs to rise much more quickly than core inflation. If we are accounting for 2.5% core inflation, we expect healthcare to outstrip it at 6-8%! The challenge increases when you consider that this rate will exceed the increases to Social Security, pensions, or other sources of retirement income. The story of healthcare has yet to be told in the United States, as rising costs from one administration encounter a different president's priorities. Regardless of who is in the White House, however, health care costs are *going* to rise—quickly—and they will be a significant factor in your retirement.

As we will talk about later in this chapter, health problems are likely going to happen—if not to you directly, to your spouse. That is not being negative; it is all too realistic. One of the biggest unknowns for retirees is how current and future healthcare laws will affect their healthcare costs. They may need to absorb more costs over time, so it is important to work with insurance specialists to help determine if you need to carry additional coverage.

Costs of health insurance just prior to age 65 is very expensive. Often, people will continue working (even in a job they do not like) simply because they cannot afford the healthcare expenses before Medicare and Medicaid kick in. Some clients have arranged their finances in such a way so as to seem poorer off and have used different state and government benefits to counter rising healthcare costs. Studies by Fidelity and others have shown that the average cost of healthcare for couples, aged sixty-five today, will be about $285,000 over their lifetime.

Additional ideas such as engaging health experts in diet and fitness regimens can greatly increase quality of life and help defray, directly and indirectly, many of these rising costs. Meet the challenge of rising healthcare costs by maintaining sufficient coverage and doing your best to start and maintain a healthy lifestyle.

3. <u>Longer Life Expectancy</u>—Thanks to advances in medical technology and care techniques, we are living longer, more active lives. **It's not just the length of your life but the quality of your life.** Studies show that those with the resources to take care of themselves and to enjoy life tend to live longer and are much happier.

According to the Social Security administration, a man reaching age 65 at the writing of this book can expect to live, on average, until age 84.3 and a woman can expect 86.6. They are quick to point out these are just averages. Another 25% will live past 90, and 10% will live past 95. These are steady increases from previous decades, yet some studies show our longevity is actually faltering due to poor diet and other factors. Other studies show that the average could climb to 90 years of age in coming decades.

Combined with higher healthcare costs, you can easily see why this is an important consideration—for you *and your spouse*. If you retire at age 65, this means that you and your spouse can expect, on average, to live roughly another 20 years on your retirement funds...or even longer! While quality of life (and health) is not always directly related to finances, adequate financial planning can help ensure that these later years do not have to be subject to a lower quality of living due to inadequate funds for medications, treatments, equipment, additional health experts, and more. We suggest focusing on *quality of life*. No one wants those extra years to be spent in poor health, so this should add even more incentive to exercise and eat right now so that you can enjoy the fruit later. Diet and exercise are two of the biggest factors, so consider adding some fitness-related

expenses to your retirement planning and adjusting your lifestyle today.
4. <u>Inevitable Market Fluctuations</u>—We have already talked about this to some extent, but it is worth revisiting in this context. Market fluctuations can be a challenge to retirement, but long-term investing takes these changes into account. We like to educate our clients about these rises and falls so they will not be taken by surprised or think it is unexpected. Instead, we teach the keys to financial success that we just discussed earlier in the book and we design a distribution strategy that helps them visualize their long-term strategy even in a volatile market.

A big way we hedge against market fluctuations is by having different "buckets" of money and investments we map out in advance. We will discuss this more in another chapter, but the short version is that we suggest having four categories—your checking, Tier I Short Term Money, Tier II Intermediate Money, and Tier III Long Term Money. Each of these pools of resources play a different role, and by using the first ones to hedge against market fluctuations that more prominently affect the Tier III fund, you can ensure you always have available cash while also getting the best return on your money.

Market fluctuations do not have to be a source of worry and concern, and in fact the best method still follows the "stay on the train" philosophy we discussed earlier. This challenge does not have to threaten your retirement, because you can use sound planning and logical decisions to navigate market volatility.

Planning for the Unexpected

While it is true that we do not know what the future may hold, we actually *can* account for unexpected events. Actuaries have known for years that things have certain likelihoods of happening over time, and they plan and charge rates accordingly. While we do not expect you to become an expert actuary, you can be more aware that some things are possible—even likely—to happen during your retirement.

1. <u>Medical Crisis</u>—We already talked about the generics of rising healthcare costs, but we also should discuss the issue of specific health events. While you may not ever know that an unexpected medical crisis is coming, it is very likely that at some point during your retirement you or your spouse will experience a medical crisis. Whether related to ongoing health issues such as high blood pressure, heart disease, or diabetes, or a sudden problem that is completely unexpected, a medical crisis can take you by surprise.

    As stated above, make sure you have sufficient coverage. Also, account in your source of available cash enough to meet deductibles, because a single medical crisis will not only hit your deductible, it is also likely to hit your max out of pocket expenses for the year. Also consider that a significant medical crisis can force a retirement at older ages, so stay on top of your health concerns, and if you have medical issues, plan accordingly as you are able. We typically suggest getting long term care insurance.

2. <u>Divorce During Retirement</u>—We discussed relationship dynamics early in the book, but we are going to revisit it briefly here. Divorce during retirement is not unheard of, but it is much less common than at other life stages. In our experience, generally a couple tends to favor the problems they know than the possibility of being alone or dealing with other (potentially worse problems) from finding a new spouse. However, should divorce effect your retirement, a good financial advisor can help not only to handle the division of retirement assets but to help preserve as much of your savings as possible so that the divorce does not cost both of you your standard of living. If you are concerned that this problem may impact you, conservative marriage counseling is a much less expensive solution than going through a costly divorce and can be very effective preventatively. You would likely not hesitate

to get a professional involved in your physical health if you expected a problem; similarly, if you suspect a relational problem, a professional may be just the help you need to keep your marriage healthy.
3. <u>Natural Disasters</u>—Natural disasters can be totally unexpected and freak random events, or they may be a seasonal threat where you live. Residents of the West Coast may face year-round earthquake or wildfire dangers, whereas the central United States may see tornadoes kick up whenever hot and cold air mix. The Gulf Coast faces hurricane season each year, and Nor'easters can batter the upper Atlantic and New England states mercilessly, as they have done just before the writing of this book. No matter where you live, these threats have been calculated for years, and flood, earthquake, fire, and other insurance products may be available depending on a wide variety of factors. Work with your financial advisor and insurance agent to see how much of what coverages are right for your location to protect your assets.
4. <u>Supporting Loved Ones</u>—From providing care for elderly parents to having kids come back to live at home after their own struggles, retirement-age couples may find themselves sandwiched between two generations that may potentially need their help. The biggest question we hear is "How much can I afford to help?"

According to a recent Pew Research study, some 15% of Millennials are living at home, which represents a rising number compared to members of Generation X. A similar trend includes increasing numbers of college graduates who are moving back home after college—regardless of whether or not they land professional jobs using their degrees. While "failure to launch" and tight job markets can sometimes play a role, sociologists are still exploring all the factors driving kids to come back or just stay at home, and you may need to discuss these possibilities with your financial advisor.

These more risk-averse generations are more conservative, and they are driven to get a high-paying job with as much security as possible. They want a lot of emotional support and are not confrontational because they grew up in times of a lot of tremendous financial uncertainty. They watched their parents struggle with horrible financial times, losing their jobs, and often losing their investments, and they need financial products they can count on. Many of them are young now, but they are the clients of the future, and good investment institutions will provide ways of helping clients like them. We have developed our Guided Wealth Products to help clients such as the younger generations who are used to using online tools.

5. Early/Forced Retirement—Though we hope this does not happen, sometimes issues come up in a company or our personal lives that may force you out of work and into retirement early. In cases like these, it is possible you will be under a non-compete or other agreement that limits your ability to engage in consulting. The one advantage to this situation is that for those asked to retire early, a severance package may be part of the early retirement.

One client we have worked with taught at a highly respected private school for 35 years. Loved by his students and faculty alike, he was laid off...and diagnosed with Alzheimer's just a few months after he quit work. He passed away about six years later, and the entire process was devastating for both him and his family. His wife had not managed to collect as much of a retirement fund as he had, and the challenge became how to take care of him at home so he would not have to go to a nursing home or assisted living facility.

6. Needing Long Term Care—None of us want to accept the possibility that we may at some point require long-term care. The idea of needing more help than a spouse or other loved ones can offer is unappealing and even frightening, yet it is a distinct possibility. This is a dual issue, including both the emotional difficulty of dealing with a long-term health issue, and the financial challenge of paying for long term care. And

every indication is that, due to increased life expectancy and the quality of medical care, more and more retirees may face this challenge.

One client we have worked with powerfully illustrates the value of long-term care insurance. While doing his taxes, his CPA contacted us about a form. While we talked, he told us that our client had spent $107,000 in health and nursing home costs just in one year—and this is in no way extravagant. And this was not the first year that cost had been so high. (At the writing of this book, the average cost of a private room in the US is over $8,000 a month,[6] and according to *Forbes* Americans underestimate the cost of in-home long-term care by almost 50%.)[7]

We had suggested that he take out a long-term care policy, and he agreed. Had he turned down that policy, he would almost certainly now be penniless.

No one likes to think of the possibility that we or our spouse will have to spend a prolonged period in a nursing home, but we must acknowledge it is possible. Strongly consider getting long-term care insurance. If problems arise, it can defray a great deal of the cost and protect your retirement funds from excessive withdrawals. One client, whose wife was diagnosed with lung cancer, shared with us after her death that having the long-term care insurance made all the difference in the end. It allowed her to stay at home during the final weeks since the insurance paid for all of her home health care.

7. <u>Scams & Fraud</u>—Scams that prey on retirees are increasingly common, and they are not always online or on the phone. We always suggest taking the time to become aware of the cons going on in your area and that are common online or at free luncheons (sometimes they are not just trying to sell you a

---

[6] https://www.genworth.com/aging-and-you/finances/cost-of-care.html
[7] https://www.forbes.com/sites/nextavenue/2016/05/10/americans-estimates-of-long-term-care-costs-are-wildly-off/#130f2ccc5180

timeshare). However, there are unscrupulous individuals who will also try to push unwise or fraudulent investments and other inappropriate things on retirees, such as indexed annuities.

Some of the most common scams include Medicare rip-offs, fake IRS phone calls, identity theft, people posing as relatives asking for money, disreputable online prescription drugs, Ponzi and pyramid schemes, and others. Regardless of the details of the scam, these predators are out to steal hard-won retirement income, they do not play nicely, and they nearly always prey on retiree's fears of losing their principal. Avoid these challenges by doing your homework, staying aware, taking precautions, and working only with licensed, reputable investment advisors with firms that have good ratings and by utilizing tools such as the SEC, FINRA, and the Better Business Bureau. We'll go into more detail about picking a financial advisor in chapter 9, and we strongly advise you to call your financial advisor when any questionable item comes up. Going into detail on these traps is not within the purview of this book, but you may want to visit our website, www.F-P-R.com, for further reading on this topic.[8]

8. <u>Death in the Family</u>—Together with needing long-term care for ourselves or a spouse, a death in the family is probably the biggest, most difficult crisis you may face during retirement. We mentioned caring for aging parents, but the cold hard truth is that eventually we all end our time on this Earth and step into eternity. We all hope our loved ones have hope and faith, but those who remain behind face difficult challenges.

Aging parents may not have life insurance policies in force by the time they pass, and depending on their financial situation, they may not have available assets to cover the costs of a burial or cremation. Some insurance policies may allow

---

[8] https://www.investor.gov/introduction-investing/retirement/avoiding-retirement-fraud http://www.finra.org/investors/early-retirement-seminars-101-smart-tips-spotting-retirement-scams https://money.usnews.com/money/retirement/aging/articles/2018-05-09/10-financial-scams-to-avoid-in-retirement

you to have benefit riders for dependents on your own policy, but you may have to cover costs from your own available funds. If you know your aging parent has failing health or that you are the only or primary person financial responsible, talk to your advisor about planning for this possibility.

Having adequate life insurance in force on you and your spouse can prevent a great deal of financial hardship in the event one of you should pass before the other. You can review your coverage needs with your financial advisor and insurance agent to ensure you have adequate coverage on yourself.

The ultimate loss is likely that of a parent losing a child. No insurance policy will ease an event like this, yet even through that nightmare scenario, adequate coverage can help ensure that financial problems do not add to the incredible tragedy. Again, benefit riders to your own life insurance policy may be available. And as difficult as the discussion may be, talking to your adult children about the need for life insurance is a very important conversation to have and is a way for you to pass on important information you have learned about insuring against financial risk.

Managing Risks

"Risk tolerance" is a term you may hear in investment circles. Your risk tolerance directly reflects your overall confidence in the market and the market variability that you are willing to withstand. People with low risk tolerance do not handle market fluctuations well; they feel the need to sell when things start looking bad. Conversely, people with higher risk tolerance are willing to ride it out.

Risk tolerance is often influenced by a number of factors, including things such as the type of investment, the amount invested, the purpose of those investments (long or short term, etc.), and the availability of cash in circumstances such as a down economy. Our three-tier investment system, which we will describe in more detail in the chapters to come, is partly designed to help manage risk tolerance.

Phillip Bell, CFP®, James K. "Skip" Nichols, ChFC, CLU, Donna Maddox, AIF®

We talked about coming to terms with behavioral finance as a key to financial independence in chapter two, and this is where knowing yourself and your spouse can be especially important. If you both cannot handle the higher risk and higher rewards without panicking and selling early, instead of staying on the train, it will be harder to earn the higher returns. This is one of the major reasons we advocate "out of sight, out of mind"—if you're not constantly watching the market and your investments, you are less likely to panic and make a poor decision.

If you assume an average rate of return of 5-6% and core inflation is at 2.5% your adjusted rate of return may be between 2.5-3.5%. If you are able to tolerate more risk and your accounts are averaging 8-12%, your accounts will grow just that much more quickly. As long as your distribution rate falls within 3-4 percent of your total portfolio, your accounts should continue to make money while also generating some of the income you need. As those accounts generate returns, you then periodically move some resources into other "buckets" of spendable money, not touching the long-term principal and instead living off the interest. In this way, savvy investors leave an inheritance to their children while still living a comfortable lifestyle.

For those who are more risk averse, lower-return investments can still produce income, but you must adjust your distribution strategy to accommodate the lower rate of returns. Your goal or strategy must be to find the level of risk you are comfortable with and then make the best out of it.

Risk tolerance appears to be based on personality type. Education can help, but most people seem pretty set with what they are and are not comfortable with. Some individuals in their eighties are just fine with risking more, whereas some studies show that Millennials are the most risk averse generation since the Great Depression.[9]

Remember, it is possible to be too conservative and not generate enough returns. So, find out what you are comfortable with, learn

---

[9] https://www.investopedia.com/articles/investing/070815/are-millennials-risk-averse-or-risk-takers.asp

about the market, risks, and rate of returns, and make use of the perspective your financial advisor has gained in his or her profession to maximize your rate of return, overcoming the challenge of risk.

Obviously, these are not the only challenges to retirement. We could fill a whole book with nothing but the obstacles we must overcome, but that is not the focus of this book. Instead, now that you understand some of the difficulties you will face, we want to move on to helping you assess your current financial health for yourself. There are many tools available to model different "what if" scenarios, and sitting down with a financial advisor can help a great deal, but let's start by exploring the "bucket" system we have talked about as well as categories of investments, asset allocation, and other issues that will help you enjoy a financially healthy retirement.

Chapter 5
Assessing Your Financial Health

When you begin the process of planning for retirement, it is important to go through a discovery process. You need to understand your own economic situation, and it is not dissimilar to the discovery process an attorney goes through for a client.

An in-depth discovery of your finances—your problems, your background, your strengths, your weaknesses, your assets, your liabilities, your goals, and much more—is a vital step. We always do this with our clients, but you can begin it yourself, and the results are always educational. Perhaps your family was always in debt, and that was your experience growing up, and therefore you are overly conservative and unwilling to take risks. Maybe you are not a very good saver or you tend to make emotional financial decisions, so you need to work on planning for the future in a more logical, ordered fashion. Whatever it is, the point is never to cast blame or point fingers. Instead, a good discovery process can help you see where you excel and where you need help.

In Skip Nichol's book *Roadmap to Financial Freedom*, he covers the path to a financially free future, and we highly recommend using that resource as well as this book. Here is what the steps look like so that you can bear them in mind as you begin to assess your financial health so that you can do your discovery and other steps with these goals in mind.

Phillip Bell, CFP®, James K. "Skip" Nichols, ChFC, CLU, Donna Maddox, AIF®

We will use questionnaires and other tools in the back of the book to help you. When we do a financial plan with our clients, we do a much more advanced version of the questionnaire, but it is our desire to introduce these things to you now so that you can be thinking of them over the next few chapters, leading up to creating your own retirement budget. The financial plan is your roadmap leading up to retirement and beyond; therefore, the information you provide is critical to creating a useful tool. For example, Joe and Marsha were considering selling their current home and buying something larger. Their two sons were at an age where they felt it would be beneficial to have the additional space. We discussed how much they were considering for the new home and what the monthly payments would be. It would mean that Joe would have to reduce his current 401k contributions, so we suggested building that scenario into their financial plan. The results showed that with the reduced 401k contributions, they would have to work six years longer in order to be able to retire with the same income objectives. They decided to stay in the current home since staying on track for retirement was more important to them.

Get to Know Your Finances

When we sit down with our clients, the biggest thing we do at the beginning is listen to them describe what is important. We like to understand who they are, what they are afraid of, and what their biggest priorities are.

So let's do that together. You can write down your answers for yourself.

1. **What is the most important thing you are looking forward to in your retirement?** For some it is being near their grandchildren. For others, it might be the ability to travel. Generally, everyone wants to be comfortable and enjoy this time.
2. **What are some things that are important to you currently that you do not want to lose in retirement?** If you like to spend time at the lake, take yearly vacations, or buy or lease a new car every couple of years, it is important to build these desires into your retirement plans
3. **What is your biggest financial fear?** For some it is losing all their money in a stock market crash. For others, it is not having enough, whether because of unexpected expenses or that they could not save enough. Whatever the case, there are ways for addressing these fears.
4. **Has anything happened in your past that you know negatively affect your financial decisions today?** Perhaps you, or your parents, went through a bankruptcy, lost retirement savings, or didn't make enough to retire well. It is important to come to terms with your past...so you can see how these things will impact your future. Some of our clients have experienced health issues that have resulted in high medical and long-term care expenses that been financially devastating. We strongly advise our clients to have a plan to pay those expenses that are not covered in standard health

insurance policies or Medicare. These long-term care expenses are covered either through Medicaid, self-pay, or with an insurance plan specifically designed for long-term care. Medicaid is available only after you have "spent down" your assets to a minimum level. This can leave the surviving spouse in a financially desperate situation. This is why we believe it is critical to have a plan in place for this potential risk.
5. **What are your spending habits?** Do you save well, or do you tend to spend as much (or more) than you make? How have you handled debt?
6. **How much are you currently bringing home and used to living on?** This is a very important consideration. Many people think that they will be able to spend less in retirement, but you must carefully consider if that is realistic and weigh it against your current income. In order to maintain your standard of living, you will often need to maintain your income post-retirement.

It is impossible to go through the entire discovery process in a book like this, but hopefully these can help you begin the process for yourself. Ultimately, a good financial advisor will help you feel comfortable and will ask you these and many other questions as he or she gets to know you and your needs and peels back the "layers" of your wants, needs, and dreams.

Unfortunately, we cannot get to know you in a book. However, we can take the next few pages to begin sharing what has worked for us and our clients and what we teach them about handling money. It all begins with handling debt.

Build Your Available Cash

While we like to get people started saving while still paying down debt, as we mentioned the emphasis will be on getting rid of the debt as quickly as possible. You may begin to contribute to retirement funds now (remember, compound interest works best over time), but if you have a lot of debt we may recommend that you put about 70% of the money you have available to save toward knocking down debt and 30% toward retirement funds.

However, you *only* start paying down debt and saving *after* you have established a pool of sufficient cash to meet your immediate needs and a few months' worth of expenses. You must first establish this available cash. If you put everything you have toward paying down debt and some retirement savings, what will happen if you have an unforeseen expense? The debt will go right back on. For working individuals, this supply of cash may start with only $1,000, but as quickly as possible you want that fund to contain three to even six months' worth of money. That way, even in the event you were to lose your job, you would not immediately start racking up debt and you'll be able to handle unforeseen expenses without too much drama—or debt.

Create A Plan to Get Out of Debt

As we learn about our clients and what they want to accomplish, we first need to know where they are in their retirement process. Perhaps you have just begun to think about retirement and you are deciding to start putting money away. Maybe you are getting closer to retirement age, and you are concerned about your debt burden. Or it could be that you are well along the way and just doing a checkup to make sure you're doing the right things. Wherever you find yourself along the journey, it is never too late to begin planning for your future. Whether you have a lot of debt or little, and regardless of how much you have to contribute to your retirement funds every month, you can begin taking steps forward to a bright future.

Each person is so different, but generally speaking, we look at things like debt first. If you have a great deal of debt, your first priority often looks like paying it down, because typically the interest rates on your debt may be higher than the returns on certain investments. Your money will work hardest for you if you first clear away what is holding you back.

You may not have thought of this, but it is possible to over-contribute to your retirement funds, which we will talk about later in the book. For now, consider this: the power of compound interest works both ways. If you have a lot of debt, it is working against you. Unsecured debt is more likely to have higher interest rates, and it is especially insidious. Just look at how long it will take to pay down your debt if you only make the minimum payments! (At least they have to show you that now.)

Look at the type of debt you have. Unsecured, high-interest credit cards are the worst. Other debt may be tied up in things such as your cars or house. If you are deeply in debt, you may need to be more aggressive in your debt elimination strategies. If you sacrifice some now, you can reap greater rewards later.

Consider moving high-interest credit cards (often 13-20%!) to a card with a short-term (six months to one year), no interest period. Typically a 3% fee may be charged, but this technique will often save a lot and allow your same credit card payment to apply entirely toward your principal.

Some areas offer debt counselling via non-profit organizations like Consumer Credit Counselling Services. They are able to negotiate directly with credit organizations to accept a lower fixed interest rate on the unsecured debt and set up a payment plan that will eliminate the debt in five years or less. This allows individuals to enter into a manageable repayment program and avoid bankruptcy.

Understanding Retirement Savings 101

We will not spend too much time here defining terms, but we want to provide a quick primer for you if you need this information. Here are a few of the most common retirement accounts:

- **401(k)**—One of the most common retirement savings account is the 401(k). Designed to be a tax-advantaged way to save money, with the help of your employer, this is an excellent choice for one simple reason: your employer may match your contributions up to a given amount. That contribution is incredibly powerful and a huge asset to take advantage of, since it is essence *free money*. Set it up so it automatically comes out of your paycheck—remember, out of sight, out of mind.

- **Health Savings Account**—We mentioned the importance of planning for expected rising healthcare costs and unexpected medical crises in the last chapter, and these savings accounts are an excellent way to pay for those expenses. Best of all, HSAs are tax-deferred. You can even pay medical expenses out of pocket and reimburse yourself at a future date. Most have debt cards for drawing on the funds, making them convenient as well.
- **IRAs**—There are a variety of IRAs (individual retirement accounts) that may fit your needs, including those of you who are self-employed. They can be invested in mutual funds, stocks, bonds, etc., and can have a range of returns. IRAs have many details and stipulations we will not get into right now, such as when they are tax-deductible or not and what age you must be before you should draw from them, but you can read up on them further or talk to your financial advisor about what IRAs might be best for you.[10]

    Today, traditional IRA's allow individuals to contribute $6,000 per year, before taxes, into a tax-deferred investment. If you are 50 or older, there is a "catch-up" provision that allows you to contribute an additional $1,000 per year. The traditional IRA gives you an immediate tax benefit in that you are able to deduct the contribution amount from your taxes for the year in which you invest. At retirement, 59 ½ or later, your withdrawals are 100% taxable.

    Roth IRA's offer the same contribution limits and catch-up provisions. The main difference is that you are contributing after-tax dollars that grow tax-deferred. You don't have the same immediate tax benefit, however when you withdraw from the Roth after age 59 1/2, everything you take out is tax-free.
- **Structured Products**—At the time of the writing of this book, the stock market is close to an all-time high. Many people are looking to or have recently become retired, and they are very

---

[10] https://www.investopedia.com/terms/i/ira.asp

concerned about protecting their principal and therefore their retirement future. One avenue we have found to reduce that risk is by using structured products. Structured products are an investment product built by and guaranteed by a very large bank. The product is built for a particular objective, usually producing income or designed for growth. Structured products also usually come with some element of protection against a certain level of stock market loss. Many structured products come with FDIC insurance. These products can be very beneficial but also can be very complicated. Professional advice is highly encouraged. Interestingly, we have seen the insurance industry shift over to using structured products inside of their annuities as the determinant for growth.

Here's an example of how a growth note might work. You have an investment built to match the growth of the S&P 500. At the end of the term, if there is a loss from the point at which you started, the investment itself will absorb the first 25% of that loss. This in effect becomes a tremendous stock market risk reduction vehicle.

An income structured note is designed to produce income, as its title implies. Let's use Steve as an example. Steve is recently retired after selling his business. He has enough but does not want to lose what he has. Therefore, Steve is very attracted to interest bearing investments. At current rates, the broad bond market will pay 2%, six-month CD's will pay 1%, and money market accounts will pay 0.2%. With those rates, Steve will quickly invade his principal. If we were to blend in some high yielding bonds and some high dividend paying stocks, then we could bump that yield over-all to closer to 3%. However, by adding an income producing structured product, we can get closer to a reasonable yield. Steve was very impressed to learn that 7.5% interest was available using several different structured products. This would keep him from touching his principal, and he was willing to accept some level of fluctuation in his account values.

An example of a CD would be a product that will give a reduced amount of investment exposure to the stock market, and in return you have a riskless investment with growth potential. With interest rates being so low, the opportunity for a 5-6% return is very attractive.

We cover these main forms of retirement savings quickly because some of the information changes as the years pass, such as IRA contribution limits, and it is better to refer to the latest information or your advisor. What *does not change*, however, is the philosophy for how to distribute your money that we cover below. This actually establishes the principles of different "buckets" of money that we have talked about before. Let's look at the categories or pools of money we advocate with our clients.

Fill Your "Buckets"

Earlier in the book we mentioned that some of investing is about managing risk. The nutshell version is this: higher yield investments almost always come with more risk, whereas lower risk investments almost always have lower yield. As we mentioned before, your investments must outpace inflation, so a certain amount of risk is going to be necessary. The art is in balancing your money and how much is in higher yield, higher risk funds and how much is in lower yield, lower risk funds. Also, you will remember that one of the keys to financial independence is having access to enough cash so that you can take care of your day-to-day expenses; after all, the last thing you want to do is to take money from one of your higher yield accounts, as these are the ones where "staying on the train" is most important.

We recommend organizing your retirement funds into four different "buckets"—four different categories that each have certain advantages and disadvantages. We educate our clients accordingly, and we help them understand that though markets may rise and fall, they eventually normalize. The trick is having access to enough money during these more difficult times so that you do not touch the principal that is generating the lion's share of your returns.

Economic downturns occur on average every 5-7 years, and those downturns last, on average, 16-18 months. We design our clients' retirement fund categories accordingly into short, intermediate, and long-term money so that they can keep their principal untouched and let compound interest do its work.

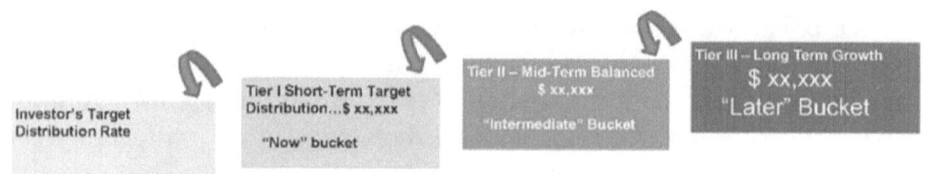

Let's take a closer look at these different "buckets" and what they do.

1. **Checking**—This is the account where money flows in and out. It is not designed to gather assets or accrue interest; it is just a temporary holding place for distributing and using money. A checking account will generate no interest, but hopefully you can get one without fees!
2. **Tier I: Short Term "Now" Money**—This is designed to provide two to four years of retirement cash flow; that is, your expected cash needs for the next two to four years (for a working person, this might be three to six months). This money accounts for various needs, both expected and unexpected. Your Christmas money may be in this bucket, but so would money in case something happens like the car breaking down or an unexpected medical expense.

    This money helps insulate you from market downturns, because you do not need to sell investments in a down market when you have sufficient cash to weather the dip (most drops in the market only last a couple of years). You keep this money in short term bonds, your savings account, a mutual fund that invests in short term bonds, etc. The key factor is that you want to be able to access this money without fees, penalties, or restrictions. This bucket earns little interest.

3. **Tier II: Intermediate Money**—This bucket contains a balance of high-dividend-paying stocks as well as bonds and perhaps annuities. This bucket is going to earn a 4-6% rate of return. For a retiree with a fully-funded Tier I bucket, this is money that will not need to be accessed for at least two years. These investments may have some fluctuation, but they are safer than the long-term money we are going to talk about shortly. It generates a greater return than the Tier I bucket but is still on the low-risk, low-return end of the spectrum. Historically, most of these types of investments have recovered their value in roughly two years if there is an economic downturn. We recommend another three to six years' worth of money be in this category. Examples of Tier II investments would include bonds; corporate, municipal, and government securities; as well as fixed or indexed annuities. These are investments that are expected to earn an average of 6-8% return annually.
4. **Tier III: Long-Term Money**—We want this bucket to earn 8-12%, but it is also subject to more fluctuation than the Tier II bucket. This is the bucket that most requires a long-term approach, because you have to "stay on the train" in order to see the gains. Thanks to Tier I and II, you should have four to eight years' worth of money available before you have to dip into this principal, and historically our clients have regained the value of their accounts in that time. Examples of this long-term bucket include things like rental properties that you may own, individual stocks, EFT's (exchange traded funds), or mutual funds that are comprised of individual stock, just to name a few.

We work with each individual investor to help determine the right amount for each bucket and to suggest the makeup for each bucket. Because a well-diversified portfolio has historically proven to be the most successful for investors, this structure has worked very well both for us and our clients (as well as investors all over the world), and we think it is the best way to break up your retirement funds rather than betting big and hoping to come up lucky.

So if the power of compound interest is so great and we want to start putting it to use as early as possible, many people wonder why they shouldn't just jump straight to contributing to the buckets that will make them the most money. If you already have some of these buckets filled, you may be able to skip ahead. But for those who are early on in the journey of saving for retirement, there really aren't any short cuts. In fact, you can actually over-contribute to your retirement, and we'll show you why.

Don't Over-Contribute too Early

Each person's financial situation is different, so a one-size-fits-all mentality does not work for our industry. While one person may be at the stage where they are putting more money into their long-term bucket, another may just need to shore up their immediate cash (remember, the key to financial independence is to have adequate cash available).

When Skip taught a financial class at Tulsa University, one young woman approached him to talk about her financial situation, which they were using for a class project. The assignment was to build their own financial plan, and this woman needed some extra help. Despite making pretty good income, she continually found herself resorting to credit cards for unexpected expenses, which had dug her into a hole of debt despite her income.

When they looked over her numbers, Skip found that because her company had a great 401(k) with matching and her father had told her to put money into the fund, she had been putting all her free money into the 401(k). Because she put all her available money into the fund, every time something out of the ordinary happened, she did not have the available cash to handle the situation...because she had put it all into a long-term bucket. Then she had to resort to using her credit cards, and she was effectively sabotaging her retirement by over-contributing to her retirement funding!

In this case of this young woman, she needed to first fund her Tier I "now" money—cash available to meet her needs. For a working person, this fund may be about three to six months' worth of income, and Skip recommended she temporarily reduce the contributions to the 401(k) so that she could build up that available cash and break the cycle of unnecessary credit card use.

We have found that a 15% pre-tax retirement savings including company matching is a good rule of thumb. When possible, you always want to contribute up to the matching portion offered by your employer. Otherwise, you're giving up "free" money. Beyond that, you should consider your current tax situation. If you are in a high income-tax bracket, you may want to reduce your taxable income, and the 401k is a good way to do that since you are contributing pre-taxed dollars.

If you are in a lower tax-bracket and you don't need the immediate tax benefit, you may want to look at other options, like individual savings or a Roth IRA.

What is the right timing or arrangement for you? Your individual situation will dictate that, so be sure you get good advice.

Chapter 6
How Much Do You Really Need?

When answering the question of how much you need for retirement, the answer is that we can't give you an exact number in a book. However, we can help you figure it out. The average couple will have a thirty-year retirement. Most people think they can live on 75-100% of their current income, but one of the most important factors to remember here is that inflation is constantly driving costs up—and some more than others.

For instance, while we already talked about inflation increasing at an average of 2.5%, healthcare costs are rising at a higher rate. Other costs may change over time as well, and that is why we build a financial portfolio and use advanced software modeling to help test your retirement numbers against things such as increased rates of inflation, market downturns, and unexpected purchases and expenses. These simulations are called Monte Carlo simulations.[11] Knowing if your investments are able to handle the stress of market factors is very useful information!

So how much do you really need to be content in retirement? This and others are hard questions that require some honest self-examination. Do you want a new car every two years? What if you stretched it to five? More? Do you need a luxury car, or is something new but more affordable just fine? Some people want to travel extensively multiple times a year during retirement. Domestic travel, rather than international travel, could cut those costs significantly

---

[11] https://www.investopedia.com/articles/investing/112514/monte-carlo-simulation-basics.asp

while still giving you the travel you desire. How much a year do you want to be able to give to your children or other family members and friends? What about charitable giving? All of these and many other factors go into answering the question of how much you need—only you know the answers.

This much we can tell you: life is going to happen after retirement. We can't predict it all, but we can plan that the unexpected will happen. If you are selective in the timing of your retirement, if you carefully consider how much you need for fixed expenses and discretionary spending, and if you stick with a thought-out distribution strategy, you can shift your financial plan to a strong state rather than retiring simply because you're tired of working. Those who retire without thinking these things through often have very weak financial plans, and they often have a lot more problems with life's unexpected twists and turns. Our clients who carefully consider the timing and amounts and schedule of their retirement and spending approach their retirement from a position of strength and are much better prepared to weather life's unexpected storms.

Because the rate of returns can change dramatically from year to year, so will the amount that you can take out. Perhaps one year is not a good year to get a new car but the next is. Sticking with the general ideas of what percentage you can take out is a great way to prevent over-invading your principal. Research tells us that if you limit your withdrawal rate, you should never run out of money. In the 1990's, that withdrawal rate was around 4%. Today, with people living longer and uncertainties about inflation and market returns, that withdrawal rate is closer to 3-3 ½%.

Good conversations with your financial advisors are so important here because you don't want to neglect having fun and enjoying your retirement...only to find that your health has slipped and you can't travel or do some of the other things you want to do. The trick is balancing the freedom and the spending with the long-term view, and this is probably one of the biggest ways a good advisor can help you.

Everyone's situation is a bit different, but when we sat down with Keith and Linda, we wanted them to have a solid understanding of the long-term implications of retiring early. Keith had retired from a government job a few years before, and Linda had continued to work as a nurse. She was starting to experience some health issues, so it was important to both of them to be able to enjoy life now while they still were in relatively good health.

Linda was 64 and not yet Medicare eligible, which meant they would have to absorb that cost. Fortunately, she was covered under a retirement healthcare plan that Keith had with his former employer. That was a huge savings for them and meant that Linda was able to retire a year earlier. Their home was paid for and they had no other significant debt, so they were able to live off of his pension and Social Security. Linda was able to wait until full retirement age to begin drawing her own Social Security benefits.

Rising Medical Costs

Earlier in the book, we talked about the rising costs of healthcare. However, this is such an important topic, it is worth revisiting. As of the writing of this book, health insurance is likely to cost around $12,000 for a couple per year. If you retire in a decade, that cost may be $24,000, so as you plan for retirement taking these rising costs into account is very necessary.

And that's not even counting out-of-pocket medical expenses. Over the course of your retirement, even healthy individuals are likely to have unexpected medical costs, even if they're only for tests that rule out real healthcare problems. Accurately estimating rising healthcare costs are one of the biggest factors in determining how much you'll need for your retirement.

Depending on the age at which you retire, you may or may not be eligible for Medicare. If you're not, bridging the gap between employer-paid healthcare and what you pay for yourself may be expensive, so take factors like this into consideration and speak with an insurance expert as you near your retirement decision. In fact, bridging this gap can be one of the biggest early retirement expenses for our clients and can sometimes sway when individuals decide to retire.

Not everyone's situation is like Keith and Linda's, with respect to health insurance. Oftentimes, individuals have to make the decision to continue working in order to keep the employer-sponsored healthcare coverage for themselves and/or their spouse, since the monthly cost of a basic plan, even with a high deductible, can range from $600 to $800 or more.

There are circumstances in which you can structure your income in a way that makes you eligible for subsidized healthcare benefits, greatly reducing your out-of-pocket expenses and making early retirement possible. This is a strategy that you should discuss with your financial advisor to see if it applies to you.

General Living Expenses

When running our financial projections, we have a large category that makes up the bulk of your costs, General Living Expenses. This includes things like your mortgage, food costs, car payments, utilities, and so forth—the very ordinary, daily expenses we all have. Most of these are expected to increase at the current rate of inflation, so in a decade it's likely that your utilities, for example, may be running you 25% more than they do today.

Breaking this down realistically is vital. How does the amount you need today compare to what you'll need in your first years of retirement? After ten years? Twenty?

Occasionally when we run these numbers, between Social Security, income from things like rental properties, and pensions, a family may have more income than they require to meet their expenses. But much more often, there's a shortfall. It's important to remember, as well, that, while we are projecting living expenses to increase at 2.5% per year, we know that Social Security payments will most likely increase at only 1.5%. Pension payments are often fixed, so there is no increase at all. Therefore, your core living expenses are increasing at a faster rate than your income. When this happens, which is much more common, we begin drawing on investments at retirement.

Perhaps you need $100,000 a year at the beginning of your retirement, and after your pensions, social security, and any other income, you require an additional $15,000 a year. You will need a distribution strategy that illustrates how quickly you can take out of your investments to cover the shortfall…yet preserve enough principal in your investments so you continue to generate the returns you need over your lifetime. If you're in your 80's and depleting your account quickly, it's a very different situation than if you're depleting it too fast in your 60's.

Discretionary Spending

Discretionary spending is the money above and beyond the basics—everything from travel to money given to your kids. When we create a financial plan, we break down the individual sub-categories, but the key here is using your budget to determine how much you want to be able to spend beyond your necessary expenses. Yes, living on a budget is arguably even *more* important after retirement than before!

The freedom you have to enjoy hobbies and travel does not mean that you can simply spend all you want. After you know how much you need, you'll know how much you can afford to use for optional items, like a trip for the whole family to the Bahamas! In order to figure out how much you'll have left, let's look at the major expenses that you'll be dealing with.

Often this is a process of trial and error. We begin with the assumption that you need a certain amount to cover necessary core living expenses. You can then add additional goals like travel, home improvement, gifting, etc., and assign a dollar amount to each goal. We build this into the financial plan, and the program will tell us if—based on your income and assets—you can successfully meet all of these objectives. If not, then we modify the goals.

Once you have arrived at a successful plan, keep in mind that these discretionary spending items are not fixed and can be adjusted. We remind clients that they need to remain flexible about their spending. In a year where market returns are not as good, you will want to consider postponing that vacation or the remodel that you had planned. Decisions like this will help to extend the life of the plan and help you successfully reach all of your goals.

One couple we worked with retired with a good financial plan, and about a year into their retirement, they contacted us for a meeting. They had decided that they wanted to remodel the kitchen—and they wanted to spend $40,000 on it. This was *not* in their financial plan. Showing them the long-term impact of taking out a large lump sum helped them to understand that they should either postpone the project or look for other ways to finance it.

The financial plan you create needs to have the goals built into it from the beginning. You don't need to know you're going to want to remodel your kitchen, but you do need to pre-decide how much money you want to be able to spend in a given year on any random thing such as remodeling. That said, we understand that not everything in life can be anticipated. The value of the financial plan is in its ability to illustrate the impact of changes to the original plan. It is your roadmap.

Additional withdrawals will invade your principal and will put the plan at risk. Life is going to twist and turn, but you can expect some of that—you're going to want to travel, you're going to want to give some money to your kids, and you're going to want to keep the house looking nice. How much do you want to be able to spend on those things and others in a year?

This is not a step to speed through. Don't just show up to a financial meeting with your advisor and spit out a number; carefully consider it. Look at your prior years of spending history. Think about the condition of your house, your kids, or your travel desires. Weigh those things against your more fixed anticipated expenses, and decide how much you can afford to spend.

How quickly you pull money out of your accounts is called your distribution strategy, and it is a very important aspect to consider. We'll take a closer look at next.

Distribution Strategy

Research tells us that if you do not take out more than 3-4% of your total assets, you will likely not run out of money and your account will continue to grow. This is generally true for those who have diversified accounts and are getting higher rates of return from that fourth "bucket" and who weather economic downturns without tapping those funds. If you take out more than this—say 5-7%—unless you are getting spectacular returns, over time you will start to pull out too much of your principal. Your account would then start to deplete because you are taking out too much principal for the account to maintain and grow and you risk running out of money.

When we build a financial plan, one of the assumptions—besides how much is needed for living expenses, healthcare, inflation, etc.—is about what we want the long-term rate of return to be. This is a complicated component that involves understanding your investment objectives and risk tolerance, which we have discussed previously. Too much in these higher-yielding accounts and you may be overexposed during an economic downturn; too little, and you won't be generating the returns you need to outpace inflation and meet your needs. It is a delicate balance.

One couple needed to take around $100,000 out of an account that was once a $750,000 account. But that was before the market took a beating in 2008 and reduced the account to perhaps $500,000. In talking with us, we convinced them to spread the withdrawal out, and they took it as a loan against their investment account. Yes, they were paying 5% interest, but they were able to get much higher returns on their investment accounts. This left their funds intact to grow during the economic upswing we enjoyed as the market rebounded. Six or seven years later, they were able to pay off the loan with the profits from their investments, and it was like the withdrawal hadn't even happened.

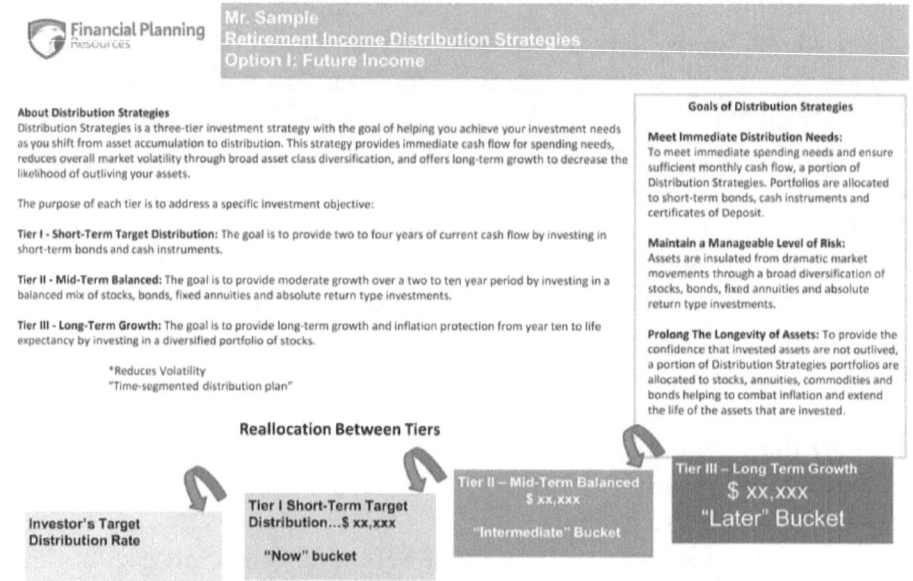

Sequence of Returns

When you take money out of your retirement funds can make a great deal of difference. We're not just talking about your age here, though that's a factor. The market's situation at the time you retire can be so important as to make or break your retirement plans.

Called your sequence of returns or sequence risk, when you begin withdrawing and what funds you draw from are both very important to consider. The difference between retiring under a bull or bear market can heavily influence your risk. For example, if you decide to retire during a bear market, your portfolio may be much weaker than it would if you wait to retire until after the market has corrected in a couple of years.

Charting a Course to the Retirement of Your Dreams

Sequence of returns — BlackRock

When we start investing, we tend to second-guess our timing. We're worried that we may take losses if buying into a down market or pay too much if buying into an up market. However, the order of your gains and losses does not actually impact your portfolio during accumulation, assuming there are no additions or withdrawals. In the end, the average return will still be the same. The examples below illustrate the portfolio value over time of three different hypothetical investments which all had an average annual rate of return of 7%. All three investments ended with the same value, although they experienced different paths to get there.

Before retirement, average return matters more than sequence

Return pattern	Year 1	Year 2	Year 3	Year 4	Year 5	Av. Annual
Portfolio A	22%	15%	12%	-4%	-7%	7%
Portfolio B	7%	7%	7%	7%	7%	7%
Portfolio C	-7%	-4%	12%	15%	22%	7%

All three portfolios end at $5.4M.

This story changes as soon as you begin retirement. Portfolio withdrawals compound losses, making it harder and taking longer to recover from a portfolio decline, especially one that comes early in the sequence. The examples below illustrate the portfolio value over time of the same three portfolios from page one, but we've now added $60,000 inflation-adjusted annual withdrawals. Once withdrawals are added to the mix, even similar portfolios can have wildly different results.

Sequence can matter more than average return when withdrawing

Return pattern	Year 1	Year 2	Year 3	Year 4	Year 5	Av. Annual
Portfolio A	22%	15%	12%	-4%	-7%	7%
Portfolio B	7%	7%	7%	7%	7%	7%
Portfolio C	-7%	-4%	12%	15%	22%	7%

Portfolio A ends at $1.1M; Portfolio B at $0.4M; Portfolio C at $0.

Not FDIC Insured • May Lose Value • No Bank Guarantee
Lit No. SEQ-RET-0919   190218T-0919

BlackRock

As you can see from the graphic, these two had very different experiences. The man receives a level 7% on his investments, but the woman's sequence of returns are quite different. Though they both end up receiving an average of 7%, she comes out way ahead.

Phillip Bell, CFP®, James K. "Skip" Nichols, ChFC, CLU, Donna Maddox, AIF®

In 2007 and 2008 when the market went down 50-60%, it was a good time to delay retirement or adjust your lifestyle. It was a very poor time to be taking money out because of the sequence of returns. Since we can't control what the market is going to do, and we can only guess in our predictions based on averages and observable trends, we can only decide what to do with what we know and the evidence before us. But we can prepare people for what to expect. As of the writing of this book, we have had a great market with spectacular returns for seven to nine years, and so we know that we will be looking at a recession at some point. We want people to be prepared, because if your plan is to retire during those years, a recession could affect your plans.

We have had to sit down with people and discuss the fact that their account has not done well because of an economic downturn or another event. One client we met with had been approved for partial disability and was about to start drawing social security, but because his account had not thrived, we had to tell him he needed to lower his distribution. He was putting the long-term performance of his financial plan at risk with how much he was drawing out, and he had to make some tough decisions about what to adjust down. However, because he was willing to cut back then, his portfolio was able to recover and begin doing well.

A couple we worked with came to us with an account with about $400,000 in it. With social security and their pensions, they didn't need much every month, and they lived a very ordinary lifestyle.

Unfortunately, their grandchild got sick—leukemia. The parents had to take turns going down to Houston for cancer treatments, and our clients found themselves helping with the expenses—hotels, travel, eating out, and all the rest. Then the parents were unable to work, and the grandparents found that they were supporting their family through this difficult time.

No one could have foreseen this happening, but with all these different financial burdens, the money went very quickly. We had to have very difficult conversations with them, because in addition to the emotional drain of a sick grandbaby and the financial stress the parents were under, they soon were in financial troubles themselves—and had some tough decisions to make.

They didn't want to talk with us about the financial situation and alternatives we tried to help with, and he had lost his health, which is why he retired in the first place. And when the money was gone, they had to make some difficult calls. How would they bridge the gap between their social security and pensions and their needs?

As financial advisors, it's our job to have those difficult conversations, and sometimes people don't want to hear it. But the alternative is worse!

If the sequence of returns and the timing of your retirement can have such a big impact, what do you do if you don't have enough or it is not a "good time" to retire? Let's take the next chapter to look at the options.

Chapter 7
What to Do If You Don't Have Enough?

If, after running the numbers, we see that your accounts will deplete too quickly, you have a few options on the table. It is always better to know while you're still making plans than after you've already retired! Some hard decisions may be in order...but if you're unwilling to make them, other decisions may be made *for* you later—and they may not be good ones! Remember, working a couple of extra years may not seem very desirable now, but running out of money in your early eighties is far worse. Let's look at some of your options if you find that you do not have enough saved up yet to retire.

- **Work Longer**—This may not be the most popular solution, but delaying your retirement by even a few years may be your best option if your retirement funds are not yet ready to bridge any gap in income without over-withdrawing and depleting them prematurely. For instance, if you were considering retiring before 65, your healthcare costs would be higher, and making it through that period of higher costs could be a significant difference. Delaying retirement till 65 could save a great deal of money. In addition, each year delayed ideally means more saved, more employer contributions to a 401(k), etc.
- **Save More**—You may have a few years of saving yet before your planned retirement, and you may not want to work longer. One option is simply to save more of your available income. Contributing more to a 401(k) is obviously a great plan, but if you've maxed that out, you can still make a difference. More money saved into a long-

term, higher rate of return fund earlier can yield big differences in returns. We shared a story in an earlier chapter about a client we work with who was looking at buying a bigger house with a pool so their kids could come over to hang out with them, but when they saw the numbers, they had to rethink this. The bigger house would mean reducing their 401(k) contributions, which would mean less savings, which would result in less money in key accounts and taking more out sooner than would be advisable. The alternative was working till he was 70, so they opted to forego the bigger house and maintaining their savings—a wise long-term decision.

- **Adjust Your Spending**—Working longer may not be an option for you. Perhaps you face retirement for medical reasons, and you will not be able to save more before you're done working. One client we've worked with was forced out of his business, and his choices were limited. If you cannot work longer, yet you face premature depletion, you may have to get creative in cutting back on expenses. Perhaps you're driving a new car; the average new car payment is currently over $520 dollars. If you sold that car and bought something less expensive, you could reduce your draw—possibly a lot! Maybe it's time to *downsize* your house with the kids out on their own. In addition to a lower payment, a smaller house costs less to maintain. There are many options.

- **Get A Higher Rate of Return**—Earlier in the book, we talked about the four buckets. How much money you put into the final bucket can considerably change the returns you get most years. This may not be an option for those with a low risk tolerance, but simply changing which funds (and thus the rate of return) could change your investment returns. This option is obviously not for everyone, so be sure to have some really good conversations with your financial advisor before making big decisions about the distribution of your funds in order to learn the potential benefits and risks.

- **Save on Taxes and Health Insurance**—A review of your goals with your tax expert and insurance agent could offer unexpected saving opportunities. You may be able to increase retirement contributions by saving money in areas such as these.

Prepare for Your Future

Being prepared for your future isn't just about adding up numbers; it's also about lifestyle and habits. If you've cultivated discipline and sound financial practices before retirement, you will be better prepared for maintaining what you've saved. If you are counting on a carefree, higher standard of living after retirement but haven't practiced the discipline of living on a budget, you could be in for a rude awakening. We all enjoy the friendly, elderly greeters at places like Walmart, but none of us want to be forced into that position by having to go back to work in our golden years.

So if you have years to go before retirement, what can you do now to prepare?

- Consider increasing your savings, either into your 401k or other investments. Take all or part of each salary increase and, rather than spending it, direct it into your investment account.
- Stay out of debt. Consumer debt is one of the main reasons people have to postpone retirement.
- Postpone discretionary spending. Again, put that extra money towards your savings.

You can still live well. Decisions like this today can make a huge difference in terms of when you can retire successfully.

- **Ask Hard Questions**—Are you willing to ask yourself the hard questions? It's easy to justify things to ourselves; it's harder to be brutally honest. But if you practice it now, you'll establish a habit that pays off later.

- **Be Realistic**—Is getting a bigger house realistic right before retirement? Many people are downsizing. Our example couple from earlier had to be realistic about how much time their sons would spend at home.
- **Get Feedback**—Since we can find ways to justify unrealistic things, it's helpful to get an unbiased opinion. Some studies have shown that women make better investments than men. Is it because they're more rational? The report seemed to indicate that it wasn't about it emotion; it was because they sought outside opinions before investing. Those outside opinions can help you answer your hard questions with honest, unbiased facts, but emotional decision making is likely to derail your financial plan and leave you with results you don't want.

We have seen all kinds of people come through our office. We know that new house or new car can look very appealing and so can that trip to Paris or that new motorhome. But having the practiced strength to make the right decision will pay off a lot in the years to come. The couple we talked about earlier who decided to forgo the bigger house to keep up their saving could easily have tried to justify the expense. They asked themselves the hard questions, and they responded with frank, realistic answers. They had one son at home for just another few years and another in college. Would either of them really get that much more enjoyment from a bigger house with a pool? Probably not—both were on their way out. And a bigger house wasn't what this couple needed for their own daily living. Despite the importance they placed on family and entertaining, they were honest with themselves and realized that it was not a smart financial move and they weren't willing to face the consequences.

We have spent part of the last two chapters talking about what to do if you *don't* have enough money, but the alternative is much more fun. Thanks to the Monte Carlo Simulations we mentioned at the beginning of the chapter, we can stress-test various accounts and can project how much money they may make over the years of your retirement. With proper planning and even modest returns, many accounts can actually be made to *grow* throughout retirement.

Consider this, by properly managing and growing your account, you can not only provide for your retirement, it could also be a legacy you leave for your children, grandchildren, or the charities that are most important to you. Your smart choices and sound financial decisions can have results that change their lives and futures.

When you are in your 80s and still able to live comfortably and without worrying about daily expenses, you'll be happy that you asked and answered the hard questions. Living well now is a terrific reward for all your hard work during your career. Passing on your success to the next generation is what legacies are made of. However, are they ready for it?

This raises another important issue with regard to financial planning. Estate planning gives you the ability to provide for your loved ones in a manner that will benefit them the most.

Passing on an inheritance is a blessing, but it brings with it a responsibility. We want to provide for our children and grandchildren, but there are sometimes circumstances that require some special planning. This is where an experienced estate planning attorney can provide some much-needed guidance. (We would emphasize "experienced.") You don't want to go to just any attorney—you want someone who is experienced and knowledgeable in the area of estate planning.

No one wants to find that they do not have enough money to carry out their retirement plans. However, it's better to be honest, ask the hard questions now, take steps rather than run out of money prematurely. However, running out of funds in your retirement years is just one of the problems we've encountered regarding money. In the next chapter, we're going to look at a few troubles to look out for as you do your retirement planning so you can avoid some of the saddest things about money.

Chapter 8
The Saddest Things About Money

Money can be a blessing. It lets us do things—go places, see sites, and so much more. But unfortunately, money can also be a source of contention. Some people say that the Bible tells us that money is the root of all evil, which isn't true—it's the *love* of money (greed, which we've talked about). When we are obsessed with it, we can turn it into something other than what it is supposed to be: a help.

Some people just seem to make money—they don't stress about it or focus on it, but they seem to simply attract it and instinctively make good decisions. When we obsess over it, we make it something it's not—a savior. We can look to money to solve all our problems, and when we don't have it, we can think that's the cause of all our problems.

It is very sad when we see money pull people apart. It's why we recommend things like trusts, good lawyers, and planning ahead—when money is in the mix, it can bring out all kinds of things in people.

Perhaps the saddest thing we see is when families fight over money. This can easily happen when someone has died and left money without proper family and estate planning. Even with that, money can divide families if they're obsessed over it. Good family and estate planning is probably the best way to hedge against this kind of fighting, and naming a reliable trustee can be one of the most important choices. For families who anticipate any possible strife, picking an institutional trustee is the best option—don't make that a point of contention among siblings or others.

One family we worked with lost their mother, and the daughter who had cared for her mother the whole time she was sick was the trustee. She had taken care of her mother; now she was left to distribute the proceeds of the trust. Her brother, who wasn't involved in any of the caregiving, and her sisters, who also did not play a big role in helping their mother, all turned on her. She ended up having to get an attorney to help sort it out, and it was hard to watch—but even harder to live through.

In our experience, most of the time reasonable kids will be just fine in this process, but when they're not it can be very difficult. Those relationships may be permanently damaged because of money, and that is very sad indeed. A well-designed estate plan can remedy many problems, save families, and save a lot of expense.

Losing It

One of the saddest things about money is seeing people have it...and *lose* it. There are plenty of cautionary tales, from lottery winners gone bankrupt to pro athletes who make millions for a very short window and then end up crushed under gambling debts, ridiculous lifestyles, and hangers-on.

We aren't really trained how to handle money—especially not large sums of it. Lottery winners who take their winnings as a lump sum are more likely than average to declare bankruptcy in three to five years, and there's no evidence they're any happier than they were before winning.

Money can be an amazing thing, but when we don't know how to handle it as a windfall, it can actually be very troublesome for our lives.

One young woman who came to us after she had inherited some money from her father. She was not working with a financial advisor when she got the money and didn't understand that the money is taxed differently if it's in a trust account, for example, than if it's in an IRA. She received around $300,000, and about $250,000 of that was in an IRA. Not understanding the tax implications, she took the IRA as a taxable distribution and ended up paying a huge amount in taxes. Not working with a financial advisor or tax professional cost her around $75,000. We created a financial plan for her that picked up the pieces, but this is a classic example of how *not* getting help cost someone a great deal.

Spending Money for the Wrong Reasons

One client we worked with retired in his mid-fifties. He was on top of the world financially, but he got into a bad marriage. Her kids both had problems with drugs and other things, and they always needed money. Because he wanted to show love to his new family, he started spending money like crazy on her and her kids—remodeling the kitchen, a family trip to Hawaii, paying off her kids' debts, building a shop behind the house (including equipment) so her son could start a business (which failed miserably in a very short time). He had $600,000 saved up and a plan for how to make it work—and it vanished in three years with little to show for it. It wasn't bad markets or unwise investments; it was a string of poor emotional and financial choices. And it cost him. He had to go back to work and used the very last of his money to help make that happen.

One gentleman we worked with started with us just a couple of years from retirement. He realized he needed some help, but his wife thought a financial advisor was a waste of money. They had never been big spenders—he was a sales representative, she was a stay at home mom, and they were pretty conservative. They'd always rented, never owned, and they had two sons who grew up and went through school before getting good jobs.

While he appreciated our professional advice, he didn't always take it, and they have tended to over-spend. They are far from the worst, and they are not egregious spenders, but that can make it all the subtler a problem. He had expensive hobbies and started spending more than what the original plan allowed for. They began spending too much right after retirement, and after a life of conservative habits, they quickly formed bad habits of over-spending in retirement. Once those habits are formed, they are hard to break.

Individuals like these have enjoyed coming into retirement during very strong markets. However, we know that every five to seven years, a market correction is going to happen—the market is going to go down at some point. By over-spending now, they are jeopardizing their future.

They have forgotten to be proactive, and by the time things are dropping and they decide to react, it will possibly be too late. They'll definitely need to cut back on their spending dramatically to weather that down time, and they aren't positioning themselves for success when (not if) the next recession comes. It's important to remain disciplined and work your plan during the good times, as well as the bad.

You cannot control market fluctuations. You can, however, control your spending, but you have to be willing to make the hard decisions.

Over Giving

We talked about the balance between competing factors of generosity and greed earlier in the book. It is a delicate equilibrium we cannot tell you how to do; we can only make you aware forethought on your giving is necessary. Unfortunately, we have seen too many examples of people who end up giving so much to their kids that it hurts their retirement (mothers, we are talking to you. You are usually the ones who will give everything to help your children, even at your own detriment). This tends to happen when they put short-term needs ahead of long-term goals. Immediate crises can seem so demanding, but in some cases, these situations cost retirees later in life and perhaps weren't as urgent as it seemed in the moment.

We have seen a few different clients who have given and given and given...creating a great deal of stress on their retirement. In the past, families often put money away over time in dedicated funds for their kids—for college, for instance. Today we are seeing fewer and fewer clients who prioritize leaving a sum of wealth to their children. While our clients clearly love their children, there is a sense among many that they have prepared their children to be successful by raising and educating them. Their priority now is to successfully navigate their own way through retirement without asking for help from their children.

If, on the other hand, your goal is to leave a portion of your estate to your children, designating certain funds for your kids ahead of time may make sense. At the minimum, decide as much ahead of time as possible how much you're willing to give; we can stress-test your retirement portfolio against that level of giving in advance, and you can see how much it will affect your retirement. Sandi, a remarried widow, wanted to leave a legacy to her children at her death. She chose to use some of her current excess income to purchase a life insurance policy on her life. The policy will pay a sizeable amount at her death, which will go to her children. This guarantees her children an inheritance even if she spends down her assets during her final years.

No one wants to see their children go through hard financial times, but often times we went through those things ourselves. At a certain point, you may not be able to protect them—possibly even should not protect them. Plenty of young couples have testified that the tight financial times are what brought them together, and sometimes it is necessary for our kids to experience the real-world adult consequences of poor financial decisions and so forth. Obviously, we cannot tell you how to handle your kids; we can only warn that it is very sad to see elderly couples forced to take jobs to survive because they gave away too much.

One client had two sons who had both gone through divorces. She paid attorney's fees and incurred a lot of out of pocket expenses helping them. She was torn because, while she loved both her sons, the two divorces racked up considerable debt that she was paying with her retirement savings. She didn't want to stand by and watch her children fall off a financial cliff because they didn't have the money, but the concern was there—how much could she really afford to help? How much would it "cost" her later if she took out too much to cover the expenses?

It is vital to know how much money you can afford to use to support an aging parent or a child who returns to the nest. Other children experience financial troubles, such as divorce or health crises of their own, and you are smart to determine ahead of time how much you can afford to help rather than finding out you gave away too much and cannot sustain your retirement.

One Out of Four

One family we worked with had a four of siblings all thrown together and into conflict when a parent died suddenly, leaving behind a two-million-dollar insurance policy. Right before he passed, he made one of his kids the beneficiary of the policy in a strange turn of events, and this child was the one who came to us, bringing the siblings with her to divide the policy among them.

Each sibling received around $420,000 after taxes and a couple of other family members who got a little. It required some work because of taxes and gift limits. But we figured it out, and they all had a big chunk of change to work with.

The oldest child was married and with children, and after a few months, the money was *completely gone*. They'd paid off the house and a couple of other debts, funded some college savings for the kids, and bought a couple of vehicles—and it was *gone*.

The "golden goose" (i.e. the $420,000) was all used up. If she had invested it in a diversified stock and bond portfolio and it earned an average of 7% net per year, it would have grown to over $826,000 over ten years. In twenty years, it may have grown to over $1.6 million! Wouldn't it have been more prudent to keep the "golden goose" invested and let it grow or just remove some of the yearly income to help with payments on the debt and the house?

The second was a hard-working, industrious young man and said he wasn't going to spend it but was going to invest it all. He ended up buying a couple of vehicles, a boat, and some equipment for his business. It was right about then the skeletons started coming out of the closets—bad debts, unpaid child support and alimony, taxes, and court costs. He paid dearly for past sins, and in a couple of years all of his money was gone, and he didn't have much to show for it.

The third sibling also said she was going to invest it, but she bought a nice, big house and used a big chunk of the money on that. Two cars and helping her new husband get his business off the ground, and the money trickled away in a couple of years.

The final child was younger, and he listened to our advice differently than his siblings. He said, "If you say not to spend the money, I'm not going to spend the money." He did buy a realistic car, and he paid for college—and eventually used that to get a good job. He kept some of the money out, but he put much of it into investments. He was able to study abroad, live modestly, and pursue his dreams. By taking only a small monthly withdrawal, he has allowed his account to appreciate, and he now has *more* than when he started. His "golden goose" is still growing and paying him dividends.

It was surprising to watch this family handle their money. One may have thought that the older siblings would be more responsible, but it was their little brother who was a blank slate for our sound financial advice. He handled the windfall the smartest and has set himself up for leaving a legacy to his own kids.

Some of our most successful investors are actually financially illiterate. They get advice, and they *follow it*. They don't try to outsmart the system, they're smart enough to get help.

We all have financial behaviors that can be unhealthy. We want to try to time the market, anticipate trends, and outsmart others. But these things are actually blind spots that a good financial advisor can help you to see.

You're paying a financial advisor for good financial advice and to be a sounding board. It's our job to be impartial, see the big picture, and advise you of the full spectrum of options and help you choose which make the most sense for your individual situation. At the end of the day, the choice of whether or not you accept this advice is yours to make.

Nobody wants to talk about the disciplines of character, patience, and saving any more—but these are the very things we advise that will save you money and eventually create wealth for you. These aren't sexy topics, and they're not the latest and greatest things. They are the tried and true values that have made and kept wealth for generations. Learning them and keeping to them, whether you learn it from your advisor or another way, is the best thing you can do for your retirement.

Be Prepared

We see all kinds of investors—typically not sports stars and lottery winners—who retire and now need to handle the funds they've accumulated. Overwhelmingly, those who do well are those who have prepared themselves. Those who are prepared for the funds they'll have at retirement, who have educated themselves and who listen to sound advice, have a dramatically better experience than those who stumble their way into retirement.

At Financial Planning Resources, we feel a "process" is critical to long-range retirement planning. Those who have worked with a firm like ours to prepare for retirement and who have spent time getting ready almost always handle their funds more wisely than those who don't prepare for retirement. They're ready. They're educated. They're prepared, and the money (and the temptation that comes with it) isn't a surprise.

We use a process to build a plan. Plans are not static—they need to be adjusted and modified over time. But when we fail to plan, as the adage goes, we plan to fail.

How good is your plan? How good is your preparation? If you answer that, we can answer with a great deal of certainty how well your retirement will go financially. Those who are ready transition more smoothly, and that sets them up for an enjoyable retirement taking advantage of all that their hard work and character has built.

What Now?

But what if you're that person who walks into your financial advisor's office and tells them you're retiring in a month. You haven't prepared; maybe you're not "ready." What do you do?

The short answer is, "Get ready to learn." One way or another, you're about to get a crash course. Listen to your advisor, and you'll probably be okay. Fly by the seat of your pants, and you're at risk.

The single best piece of advice we can give you is to arrive at the amount per month that you must have—and, remember, there's a difference between what you "need" and what you "want"—and then build a plan around that. The best way to find that number is to look at your current paycheck—can you live on that? If so, that's probably about how much you'll need to transition.

Many people think they can live on less, but a quick look at your savings history will prove whether your lifestyle is compatible with the lower amount or if you are conditioned to living at the higher amount. If your paycheck has brought you $7,000 a month, you have $5,000 a month in expenses, and you have saved the remaining $2,000, you probably really can get by with closer to $5,000 in retirement. However, if you have not been saving that extra (or a good portion of it), you will have to adapt your lifestyle in order to exist on the lower amount in retirement. You're better off assuming that you need to spend more in retirement and planning accordingly than unrealistically expecting that you can make due on the lower amount and then overdrawing your account.

Not only that, it's important to be realistic about your expenses early. How old is your car? How much maintenance will be required to keep it in good running order until you have planned to replace it? How old is your house? Will it need a new roof in a few years? What if the water heater breaks? How much is in your checking? Savings? If you have a low balance, where does the money go? It's important to ask yourself all of these questions.

You may not be able to anticipate when the car will need repairs or when the heating and air conditioning could go out, but you can expect that these unscheduled expenses *will* happen at some point.

Looking at all these factors can help you determine if you're ready to retire. Go over them with a financial advisor, because they are very familiar with budgeting for the unexpected in your retirement plan, and they are impartial about what they recommend. If you're not ready or it's not a good time, they will help you determine this.

One word of caution: unscrupulous financial advisors may urge you to retire now when in fact you may be best served by waiting. The problem is, they may have a conflict of interest.

That is why it's so important to pick a person of high integrity. In fact, we believe so strongly in you getting the right help for your financial decisions, we want to dedicate the next chapter to helping you pick your financial advisor. Remember, this is more than just someone to pick investments; this is a relationship.

Chapter 9
The Fine Art of Getting Help

Finding a financial advisor is not the only way to get help, but it is what we will focus on in this chapter—why it's important, how to pick a good one from the crowd, and so forth. However, educating yourself and taking advantage of resources are also great ways to get help. Seminars, classes at local colleges, and online tools can be great assets. Individuals such as Dave Ramsey, Nick Murray, and Suze Orman, just to name a few, have great books and programs.

However, finding an ethical advisor with whom you can connect is arguably the most important step you can take as you head into retirement. Remember, it's not just about picking investments or doing math; it's about knowing you and what you want your money to do for you. When you have a friendly working connection with your advisor, and you trust that person enough to listen to the impartial advice you are paying them to give you, you gain a very valuable asset that will make and save you a great deal of money. Remember the great advice from President Ronald Reagan: "Trust but verify."

Coming Safely Down the Mountain

There are a lot of do-it-yourself individuals who have not hired a financial advisor. Some are very good at handling their finances; some are not. Many people believe they can manage their company 401(k) with a little research. The problem is that, for most people, their 401(k) may be their largest investment and, therefore, the most important from a planning perspective. It needs to be properly managed and, unfortunately, most companies offer little or no investment advice related to the 401(k) plan. This is where an experienced advisor can help provide much needed guidance.

It becomes even more important at retirement to have that professional advice to help you navigate your way through challenging investment environments that will inevitably occur. Therefore, it is more dangerous and difficult to watch over your retirement plan after you retire than before.

We like to use the example of the first Western man to climb Mt. Everest. If we asked you first who climbed the tallest mountain in the world, much of the world will answer Sir Edmund Hillary. He climbed Everest in 1954. But in reality, he is *not* the first person to successfully climb Everest—the first person summited thirty years before, but his body was not found until the late 80s. George Mallory climbed Everest in 1934, but he didn't make it back down.

Climbing the mountain can be easier than coming down. We use this illustration because saving for retirement can be easier than managing your retirement. When you are working, you have a paycheck and you have decades to go before you need the money. If the market goes down, if you're a long-term investor, you know you have time for it to recover. After you retire, you're in a more dangerous place, because you're looking at your money and wondering if it's going to be enough. What happens if the market goes down again as it did after 9/11 or the financial crisis in 2008? We know from past experiences that the market will go down. What will you do when the funds you've put aside are threatened by a market fluctuation? Will you panic?

When emotions like fear get involved—and who wouldn't be afraid if their nest egg got cut in half from a sudden drop in the market?—it's easy to behave differently than you did when you were building your retirement funds. It's easy to do the wrong thing. You can transform from the long-term investor you still need to be and into a knee-jerk reactionary.

This is where a steady head can be such a help. A good advisor is there to help you make the smart, well-thought-out choice so you respond carefully instead of simply reacting out of fear (or greed).

Elaine scheduled a meeting to discuss the purchase of a new car that she needed. It wasn't an unreasonable purchase. Her current automobile was over ten years old and, as a retired single woman, she wanted something that would be reliable. She could have taken out $30,000 from her investments and paid cash. This was her original plan; however, we suggested that she consider financing the car through her bank or the dealership and then taking a small monthly distribution from her investments to make the payments. That had never occurred to her, but she was delighted with the idea of being able to use the bank's money and keep her own invested. She was able to finance the car at a very attractive interest rate, and she will have it paid for in three years while her investments have the opportunity to continue to grow for her.

The right financial advisor will tell you if you're not ready to retire. They will tell you if you are being unrealistic. They'll ask you the hard questions, and they will look out for your best interests. So how do you find someone like this?

One of our first pieces of advice on picking an advisor is to look for a long-standing firm with a history of providing quality service to people. You don't want someone who is on his way out in a few years—not that he'd tell you—who gives you advice based on selfish motives. An advisor with a firm has the standards of the firm to live up to, which provides accountability. A lone individual may have great skills and may charge less, but you run the risk that a lack of accountability may make that person more likely to think selfishly or short term. It also raises the question of succession planning. What happens when the sole proprietor decides to retire? What happens to your account?

An established firm has more reputation for you to research than just the one individual you'll be working with—they have standards of service that their advisors must live up to. You can then expect a certain level from the firm and from the individual you will work with, and you can look at their performance as a group, as well as individually. It is important you like and work well with your advisor, but when they have a team behind them it is very valuable.

Phillip Bell, CFP®, James K. "Skip" Nichols, ChFC, CLU, Donna Maddox, AIF®

Do Your Homework

When picking an advisor, do your homework. There are many commentaries telling you what to look for, but they generally all agree on the basics.

- **Certified**—The first thing you probably want to check for is whether they are a certified CFP (Certified Financial Planner) or ChFC (Chartered Financial Consultant). The Certified Financial Planner Board of Standards (CFP) is a non-profit organization that upholds a standard of excellence that its members must adhere to. Formed in 1985, it is commonly considered a "gold standard" for financial advisors. Applicants must meet CFP's levels of education, examination, experience, ethics, and more in order to be certified. The ChFC, Chartered Financial Consultant, is nearly identical to a CFP-issued designation and is from the American College. Advisors may go with the CFP or ChFC or both.
  - **Education**: CFPs and ChFCs should have "a common body of knowledge lies at the foundation of any profession. Applicants for CFP® certification, a professional certification rather than an educational credential, must complete a course of academic study covering personal financial planning topics that financial planning practitioners have identified through periodic job-task analysis studies."[12]
  - **Examination**: CFPs and ChFCs should have "a second building block of a profession is the ability to verify that those who wish to practice the profession have mastered a certain level of theoretical and practical knowledge. For most professions, this proof takes the form of an examination. CFP Board's comprehensive CFP® Certification Examination

---

[12] https://www.cfp.net/about-cfp-board/about-cfp-board/history/certification-milestones#education

reflects a philosophical perspective that distinguishes "certification" from "education." In effect, it is a practical knowledge exam, rather than an academic test. The examination's purpose is to assure the public that new CFP® certificants have competence in the financial planning topics that practitioners have said are necessary to the practice of personal financial planning."[13]

- **Experience**: CFPs and ChFCs are required to achieve certification milestones. "CFP® certification, as a professional certification, indicates to the public an individual's ability to provide professional financial planning services without supervision, and CFP Board requires applicants to have experience in delivering the financial planning process to clients."[14]
- **Ethics**: All of the knowledge and certifications available would mean little if the individual is unethical. As such, "A fourth critical characteristic of a profession is its commitment to a high standard of ethical conduct. CFP® certificants are required to abide by CFP Board's ethical standards, as set forth in the *Standards of Professional Conduct*, and are subject to disciplinary action when those standards are violated. CFP Board's high ethical standards and its rigorous enforcement of its ethical standards, including the public release of disciplinary information, are key factors that differentiate the CFP® certification from the many designations in the financial services industry."[15]

The CFP Board requires an ongoing commitment to staying up to date and educated, including exams, thirty hours of continuing education, and more. You can also

---

[13] https://www.cfp.net/about-cfp-board/about-cfp-board/history/certification-milestones#examination
[14] https://www.cfp.net/about-cfp-board/about-cfp-board/history/certification-milestones#experience
[15] https://www.cfp.net/about-cfp-board/about-cfp-board/history/certification-milestones#ethics

check on advisors with the U.S. Securities and Exchange Commission (SEC) and through FINRA's Broker Check.[16]

However, Warren Buffett may sum it up best when he says, "Hire someone who has integrity, intelligence, and energy. If they lack integrity, the other two are worthless."

- **Sufficiently Experienced**—You always want to pick an advisor who has not only the educational background but also the personal experience to adequately manage your accounts. While we all must start somewhere, established firms will back their new advisors with more experienced mentors. Remember, the CFP and ChFC certification requirements are minimum requirements. Applying knowledge is different than simply having it, and you want some evidence that they have successfully helped others and can help you. The best situation is that they have helped enough other people they understand the market practically and may even have dealt with situations like yours before. You want to know they've seen the highs and the lows, and they'll have the patience and perspective to help you in the long term.
- **Your Best Interest**—The best advisor will look after your best interests. "Fiduciaries" are supposed to look out for your best interests, period—in *all* ways and for all of your accounts. Registered investment advisory (RIA) firms are, by definition, fiduciaries so that is a very critical thing to look for. Other advisors who are not fiduciaries are required to give advice that is "suitable" for you, which may not be for you and your accounts' ultimate best interests.
- **Get Along**—This may seem overly simplistic to say, but you want to like your advisor. You will be making big decisions with this person, so you want to feel very comfortable with this person. If you don't, shop on. You would not settle for a doctor with whom you weren't

---

[16] https://brokercheck.finra.org

comfortable with sharing personal details of your physical health, so think of your financial advisor in the same way. This is someone with whom you will be sharing some very personal details of your financial life. Therefore, it's worth taking the time to find someone whom you can trust, communicate well with, and understand.
- **Fee-Based vs Commission**—Find out how your advisor gets compensated. It will either be by upfront commission or advisory fees. In our view, there are two drawbacks to upfront commissions. First, if the compensation is all paid upfront, there may not be much incentive for your advisor to continue to serve your account. Second, what happens if the new investment you made turns out poorly after a few months and you have to sell it? Now you are out the first commission and face paying another commission.

    For the above reasons, we feel an advisory fee arrangement is better for the investor. Fees are typically charged on a quarterly basis. Therefore, the investor is not "locked-in" if he or she must sell early. Typical fees run 1.25% per year for accounts valued at $250,000 or less. For larger accounts, there should be a reduction in the fee charged. The fee arrangement provides a financial incentive for the advisor to carefully manage the investment account. In other words, if the investment grows in value, the advisor fees grow also. If the investment declines in value, the advisor fees decline as well.

How do you quantify the value that a financial advisor brings to your situation? It's a question many have asked.

With the so much emphasis on fees today, there is a temptation to measure the value-add as an annualized number. While fees are important, we believe there are other considerations.

We feel that the role of the advisor is to answer two critical questions: Are you on track to meet your financial goals and are there any blind spots that you've missed? In order to answer those questions, the advisor should engage with you in a discovery process to understand, among other things, who you are and what's important to you about money. Are there fears or concerns that you have? How to you feel about market volatility? The answers to these questions will shape decisions when your advisor is developing an investment strategy for you. Through behavioral coaching, portfolio construction, and overall wealth management, an advisor can add meaningful value to your portfolio.

Sometimes the greatest value add from an advisor is in helping investors maintain perspective, especially in challenging markets. The normal human response during these times is to abandon a well-thought-out investment plan. Research has shown that working with a financial professional can add about 3% net return to your portfolio. The chart below represents market movement from 2007 through 2019 in a balanced portfolio of stocks and bonds, a 100% bond portfolio and an account that was 100% in cash. Each had very different results. It's in times like these when guidance is needed most.

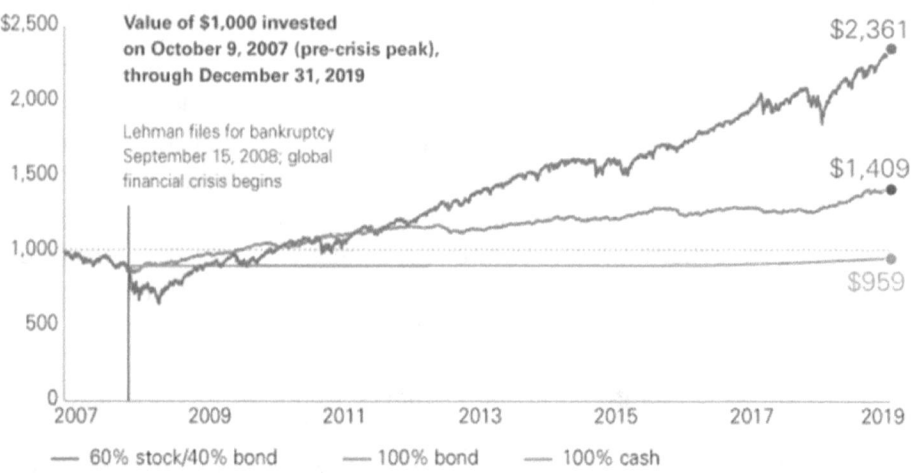

Trust is another component of this process. Hiring a financial advisor is not unlike a relationship you might have with your doctor.

You are believing that person has your best interests in mind. You are entrusting them with your financial future. We feel that it is critical to understand the things that are important to you in this process relative to the things that you may not be able to control. For example, one of the things we can't control are events that drive market volatility. However, if it is important that your advisor be responsive, you should have a reasonable expectation that your phone calls and emails are answered in a timely manner. Do you want that person to proactively reach out to you during turbulent markets? Many times, that does not happen and this is often one of the main reasons people change advisors.

In the final analysis, you need to know the things that matter to you versus the things that you can control. They are often very different, but sometimes there's overlap and that is where your focus should be.

How to Work With Your Advisor

The conversations we have as financial advisors are not always fun. Sometimes accounts under-perform. Sometimes the market takes a dive. Sometimes needs change, or people are withdrawing too much, too quickly. When these things happen, the talk can be tough. But most of the time, people understand that they have paid for expert advice that goes far beyond which funds to pick.

When you're working with your financial advisor, weigh their feedback carefully. You have paid them to look out for your best interests, and generally speaking they have a great deal of experience managing many portfolios, not just yours. However, we cannot *make* you do anything. In the end, the choices are up to you.

A Tale of Two Investors

A man came to us with a question about drawing his deceased wife's social security. He wanted to defer drawing his own but began drawing hers and thought this was the right decision, which we agreed was a wise decision.

But as he told us his life story, he explained that he had gotten a very early start in life with two kids when he was still in his teens. He finally got a good job reading meters, going from yard to yard (and dog to dog). He did this for years before getting a job inside the audit department for a lousy boss. He figured out how to work with this unpleasant man, and he worked his entire career in this department.

Most of this man's career was spent working with a friend of his who was actually a notch above him in the company. Though this other man made a little more and had a little higher level of education, they were very similar.

Both men were saving into their 401(k)s and a stock purchase plan their company had for employees. But the first man invested aggressively in his 401(k). The other man invested very conservatively with his retirement accounts, and by retirement he had $480,000 saved up.

The first man who once read meters but had invested aggressively (and had left it alone) had over *two million dollars* saved up! He had remained patient and disciplined, hadn't messed with it too much, and had ridden out the downturns, keeping his money in the market (staying on the train).

The first man simply learned the important details of managing wealth and did what his advisor suggested he do, and he will be enjoying these benefits for the rest of his life, as well as possibly leaving a significant financial legacy for his children and charities. He invested himself in learning, was disciplined with his saving, and let the market work for him by staying on the train. Our relationship with this client is a pleasure not because he just did what we suggested; it's amazing to be able to see him do well and expand his portfolio, live comfortably for years to come, and provide help to others less fortunate.

Experience Helps Make Informed Choices

One of the biggest assets we offer customers is an independent third party perspective. We are not emotionally involved, and we have a great deal of experience because we often manage multiple accounts. In the case of those who have been doing so for years, we have a considerable life experience and history of investment.

Perhaps you're considering whether to take your company's offering of your pension given in a lump sum as they're downsizing as opposed to trying to stick it out and receiving it over time. Getting to know you is a big step—are you a disciplined saver and spender? Or do you tend to make emotional financial decisions? If you have a long track history of making really good financial choices, getting it all at once may present a great investment opportunity. If you've tended to spend more freely, you may want to wait and try to get those payments made over time so the structure helps you stay on your budget.

You know you best. But when we get to know you and combine that with what we know about people, investments, the markets, and more, a good financial advisor can offer you priceless feedback and advice.

Financial advising is not just a numbers game. It's about *people*. It's not enough to find a financial advisor that's good with math; you need someone who is good with people—with *you*. Whomever you pick, choose someone trustworthy and you like, because this is a relationship that can help steer you through some of the very best years of your life. Again, remember Warren Buffett's advice—without integrity, any other positive attributes your advisor may have are worthless.

Chapter 10
Plan to Live the Highest Quality Life

A book by a Korean yoga master, *I Decided to Live Until 125*—in addition to having a funny title—actually had some real-life wisdom we want to pass on here as we wrap up the book. The ultimate idea was this: we don't have any control over how long we are going to live. However, we can plan to live with as much quality of life as possible. In this book, the author's focus was on things such as the importance of exercise, nutrition, and belief. His important concepts pertained to our physical health, life, and wellbeing.

But we'd like to apply this to your financial life. You plan to have financial quality of life just as surely as you do your physical life, and we do not plan to just accept whatever happens to us. We can plan to have the best possible life.

Focus on the Right Things

In our experience, we have noticed that people tend to focus on the wrong things.

- **Costs and Fees**—People can focus on fees and costs, for instance. Some groups will advertise low trading costs or reduced fees or the low expenses of their funds. While fees are important, *results* are even more important! If you look only at the fees, you could easily miss the fund that is performing better. Remember, the amount of money isn't the focus; focus on the percentage of return.
- **Tax Penalties**—It's also very important to look at what kinds of taxes will result from your actions, such as early withdrawals from your qualified accounts that generate

penalties or tax-saving strategies like gifting all or part of your RMD's.
- **Your Behavior**—The final thing that people overlook all too often is behavior. In many colleges, you can get a degree in "behavioral finance" studying the *behaviors* of investors and how that affects the returns on accounts. Too often we're obsessed with trying to pick the right fund or predicting the market, when in fact our behavior has a great deal to do with our success. For instance, people who invest based on fear or greed are setting themselves up for problems (and no one considers themselves to be acting greedily or fearfully even when we are). People who hop in and out will fail to take advantage of the 9.14% average history of return from the S&P 500 Index; instead, the Dalbar Study tells us they'll average 3.3%. That is not the market's fault. That is the result of behavior.
- Have a long-term vision

Guided Wealth Portfolios

More of our younger investors, Millennials and Gen X'ers, naturally gravitate to online resources when it comes to investing. Unlike their parents, they are less inclined to want a face-to-face meeting to discuss investing. They prefer an online method, and Guided Wealth Portfolios are a way for investors to manage their accounts, with or without the assistance of an advisor, using technology. All of the tools are provided to help the investor choose the appropriate investment allocation that matches their investment objectives, risk tolerance, and time horizon, with as much or as little help from an investment professional as they want, and it's all done online.

Conclusion

Congratulations! You have started your journey on the Roadmap to Retirement. If you are among the Baby Boomers, that means that you are joining about 77 million other boomers who will be retiring in the coming years—10,000 a *day* through 2030! Many are ill-prepared and depending on Social Security, but will you trust these institutions to take care of your needs throughout retirement?

We hope not!

The contents of this book can only account for the very tip of the iceberg. We could fill many books with relevant details, but not all would be applicable to you. It is our hope that with this roadmap, a guide to get you started, you now feel better equipped to start making more informed financial decisions and expand your financial education.

Your next step looks like action—taking a step. If you do not already have the services of trusted advisors, we suggest using some of the tips we've provided as the starting place for doing your due diligence and selecting *competent, qualified* individuals to help map out the detailed plans for your personal retirement adventure. We suggest developing a relationship with well-rated accountants, estate planning attorneys, and financial planners, as well as the insurance specialists who can guide you through health, life, and property/casualty questions.

We cannot emphasize enough how important it is to qualify each and every one of these individuals; we have seen too many tragedies from those who took the advice of under-qualified people. Do your homework! The internet has revolutionized how available information is and how individuals can communicate about their experiences, so take advantage of every tool to thoroughly check out each individual with whom you trust your financial future.

Phillip Bell, CFP®, James K. "Skip" Nichols, ChFC, CLU, Donna Maddox, AIF®

When you have selected the knowledgeable helpers necessary to chart out your next steps, we urge you to stay active and involved. No other individual is as concerned about your financial wellbeing as you are, so you owe it to yourself and your family to never stop learning. Continue your financial education, and then share what you learn with your family—it's the best way to make the knowledge permanent and relevant!

Organizations such as ours often offer free educational meetings to expand the knowledge of individuals in our area. These free, informative gatherings are excellent ways to get more information and grow in your financial education. If you would like more information on our meetings or how to find those in your area, please visit our website at www.F-P-R.com or email us at james.nichols@lpl.com.

Finally, God bless you as you embark on the adventure that is retirement. You have some of the best years of your life ahead of you, and it is our hope that we have helped you in some small way to have a better life!

Securities and financial planning offered through LPL Financial, a Registered Investment Advisor, Member FINRA/SIPC.

The opinions voiced in this material are for general information only and are not intended to provide specific advice or recommendations for any individual. All performance referenced is historical and is no guarantee of future results. All indices are unmanaged and may not be invested into directly.

This information is not intended to be a substitute for specific individualized tax or legal advice. We suggest that you discuss your specific situation with a qualified tax or legal advisor.

The rule of 72 is a mathematical concept and does not guarantee investment results nor functions as a predictor of how an investment will perform. It is an approximation of the impact of a targeted rate of return. Investments are subject to fluctuating returns and there is no assurance that any investment will double in value.

All investing involves risk including loss of principal. No strategy assures success or protects against loss. There is no guarantee that a diversified portfolio will enhance overall returns or outperform a non-diversified portfolio. Diversification does not protect against market risk.

This book contains only general descriptions and is not a solicitation to sell any insurance product. For information about specific insurance needs or situations, contact your insurance agent. This book is intended to assist in educating you about insurance generally and not to provide personal service. State insurance laws and insurance underwriting rules may affect available coverage and its costs. Guarantees are based on the claims paying ability of the issuing company. If you need more information or would like personal advice you should consult an insurance professional. You may also visit your state's insurance department for more information.

Examples of case studies are hypothetical examples and are not representative of any specific investment. Your results may vary.

www.ingramcontent.com/pod-product-compliance
Lightning Source LLC
Chambersburg PA
CBHW030841180526
45163CB00004B/1416